One Body

My story of trauma and survival

Sarah Lovell

Copyright © 2014 Sarah Lovell
All rights reserved.

ISBN: 1497379342
ISBN 13: 9781497379343

ONE BODY

My life has been touched by a multitude of extraordinary events. They have come to me in various ways, leaving their mark on my soul as well as my body. I have not succumbed to these terrible experiences. They have been no match for me.

Come, walk with me through what were the darkest times of a young girl's life. Experience with me the unspeakable horrors that befell my children and riddled my adult life with fear. Read how I lived through them all and still came out on the other side with a heart still able to love, a life worth living, and a fire in me to help those who have suffered the same way.

One Body gives a firsthand look at my experiences with sexual abuse, brutal domestic abuse, my own kidnapping, the brainwashing and trafficking of my fourteen-year-old daughter, the severe bullying of my twelve-year-old daughter, and our recovery from all of these horrors.

A true friend once said, "Girl, I don't know how you keep bouncing back. We should all have your strength and perseverance." Thanks, Lala.

THIS BOOK IS DEDICATED TO MY CHILDREN.

R.

Handsome boy. Well, he's a man now. He was the first, and I wish I could have been there to watch him grow, but I wasn't.

I will be there now. To help him, to guide him in his adult life. I'm sorry, Son. I love you.

M.

I would give anything to have the chance again. But I didn't deserve her. She was an angel who didn't ask to be here.

I did wrong by her, but she was given a beautiful life. I love her with all my heart. She is amazing and has grown into a beautiful, amazing, and smart woman.

I thank my parents for loving her and being what she needed because I could not.

I love you, my darling. I'm sorry.

S.

My sweet girl. You are a fighter. I love your strength and courage. You have amazed us all.

A.

You are the baby. Growing up too fast. Having to watch your life change before your young, beautiful eyes. I will teach you to live, to fight, to breathe.

1

TRAUMA 101

I grew up in the town of Bridgewater, Massachusetts. When I was a girl, we had a neighbor who had a huge German shepherd named Scout who was always chained out in the backyard. I would go out there to see him as often as I could. There was a small patch of woods back there, where I would explore and look for treasures. I would talk to Scout and ask him questions while I was on my little missions. I loved doing things like that when I was little. I went to see Scout one day, and before I got to his area, his owner stopped me and told me not go near him. At first, I didn't understand, but as I looked at him lying there on the ground and not moving, I realized he was dead. He had died from heartworm. I was so sad. The feeling that my friend was gone was the worst feeling I had felt so far in life.

I remember growing up in a churchgoing family. It was where you could go to talk to God and be happy. That was my little-girl perception of it. We went every Sunday, and I thoroughly enjoyed it…until I got a little older and everything in life began to change.

Don't we all start our lives as innocents? I want to start over, to be whole. To stay whole and unscathed by evil. Why not, why can't I? Why do these kinds of things touch the lives of children? Do they not, as beings who have never done anything to anyone, deserve a fair start?

I think as far back as I can go, and I can remember being a happy girl at times. But my strongest memories are of feeling tortured by something, of being so terrified by the dark that I would break out into a sweat. I remember staying with a friend of my mother one night and I was screaming in fear for my mom. Not because of the woman, whom I loved; I just remember being consumed by fear of something unseen. I was inconsolable and even when she let me sleep in her bed with her, I couldn't shake the feeling. I constantly had a feeling that something terrible was about to befall me.

Before age six, I had no father. His whereabouts were, and still are, unknown. All I know of him are reports from my mother. He abused her, and when she left him, he was never heard from again. I do remember one picture of him from our photo album. That disappeared after my mom married my true dad: the man who met my mom, married her, adopted me, and raised me as his own. You would think it would have made my life picture-perfect, but it didn't. I had demons, even back then.

Don't get me wrong, I loved my family and had a great life. I went to private schools; I had horses; I never wanted for anything. I loved going to my grandmother's house. There was a wall of canned goods in her basement stairway. I would find the cans of peaches and eat as many as I could before getting in trouble. Any time we went there, I would find my way to a small closet on the second floor of her house. That closet was the most peaceful place I knew. There were mysteries there. The old photos and papers that had surely been left there for me to discover. Marionette puppets and ceramic dolls were my friends. They waited for me on each visit. They made me happy. It still makes me smile thinking about how much I enjoyed those moments. I would wander around my great-aunt's house and play her piano, snack, and hang out with my cousin. I also loved it when the whole family would get together. My grandmother and great-aunt would cook up such a storm, you couldn't move after all the eating. There was pasta and the most amazing sauce made by my great-grandmother. There was an enclosed porch at the house, and all the pies and pastry would be set out there. Well, I got caught more than once sneaking pieces of squash pie and any other sweet thing I could get my hands on. There was so much food and laughing. Well, there was a tiny bit of arguing too, but my memories are still beautiful. I wish I could go back to those times. They loved me so much. I could feel it. I wasn't spoiled, but I was never hungry and never cold. My parents worked hard to make a good life for me…but the feelings of happiness and contentment would soon change.

For some reason I think about hearing crickets that night. Back then I wasn't quite so afraid, so it was likely that I had my windows open and was able to hear crickets. In those days I breathed easily in the night and fell into a deep and comfortable sleep. I would guess that I was around eleven years old.

What woke me up was the sound of my father's voice asking the man what he was doing. This man was from our church. My parents were always trying to help those who had less than we did, so they had given a homeless man from our church a place to sleep. He was drunk, I think, and was apologizing to my father for drinking his liquor, or whatever it was. He kept promising not to touch it again.

"Trust me," he said. "Just leave the bottle right here and when you wake up it will still have the same amount in it as when you went to sleep."

I could hear him slurring his words. Believing him, my father retreated to his room he and my mother shared on the other side of the kitchen.

I had gone to bed with my lights on. I'm not sure why. And I was wearing one of my tank tops.

First I heard the homeless man mumbling something to himself. His voice grew closer as he entered my room. Then I smelled him as he stood close to the side of my bed. He smelled so foul. He was filthy and had an aroma of alcohol. He began talking to me. I pretended not to hear, hoping he would leave. Then I felt his hand pulling my covers down and then resting between my legs. His breathing was getting deeper. Oh my God, what is he doing? I turned my body away from him, my eyes still closed, but he continued rubbing his fingers between my legs. Abruptly, he stood up and left the room. Was my father coming? Please let him rescue me from this terrible thing!

How could I possibly go back to sleep after what had just happened? I was so confused. Why had he just done that? Wait. His shadow appeared again in my doorway. I squeezed my eyes shut and turned toward the wall again. Oh, no. Please don't come back in!

Again he was at my bedside mumbling some more ridiculous nonsense.

"Get away from me!" I wanted to scream, but could not. I could not speak, and he could not hear my thoughts.

This time he reached his hand underneath my tights and underwear and began touching me skin to skin. His hands were rough, and they were scratching me. It was the most sickening thing I had ever felt. I tried to turn away again, but he pulled me back toward him.

"Don't you like it?" he asked.

No, I didn't want this, but I was unable to say anything. "You know you like it." He pulled his hand out, licked his fingers, and put them back inside my tights. He kept whispering, "Good night, Irene," and calling me a bitch. He was actually kind of singing it to me. I had no idea what he was talking about. I wanted to tell him to stop touching me, but I couldn't. Would he hurt me? Hurt my parents? Please make it stop! Please go away!

Finally he stopped. He said it again, "Good night, Irene," and left my room.

What an asshole.

I find it amazing that I remember nothing about the rest of the night or the next morning. I never told a soul. Not until I was over thirty and even then, only my father believed me.

How strange that it only took a few pages to describe this experience, but the trauma has stayed with me my entire life. It marked the beginning of the experiences that would change my life and how I viewed the world. I was no longer seeing things as I should. My sleep pattern changed then as well. I could no longer sleep through the night. I was always on guard and woke up at every sound. Everything I experienced after that point was tainted. Twisted even. By twisted, I mean that my perception of everything was different. I questioned other people's motives; I had learned not to trust.

As I got older, I couldn't ever settle my mind. It was always spinning, worrying about what someone else was up to and what that person wanted from me.

I felt I had to constantly plan my next move. Yet, at the same time, I was drawn to dangerous things that others shied away from. I was looking for excitement. I desperately needed an escape. I was to eventually find it.

2

HAMPTON

So much has been blanked out in my mind's attempt to protect itself, but some memories still remain. Summers were a favorite of mine as far as family goes. My family would rent a beach house and each part of the family would spend time there. I loved lying in the sun. I baked myself in the sun. My grandparents always got lobster and the sweetest fruit I had ever tasted. One of the things I enjoyed the most was the ocean. I spent so much time in the water, my lips would become purple and my fingers were wrinkly. I often sat at the edge of the water wiggling my toes in the ocean and lying on my back waiting for the waves to wash over me. My favorite was floating in the water on my back and drowning out the sounds of the rest of the world. Calls to come in and eat or go to family outings would eventually come, and I would be temporarily brought back to reality, which I didn't really enjoy because I was happiest when I was completely submerged inside my own mind. Thinking back now, I wish I could have stayed there.

Bits and pieces of the next event are all I have left. I know that I was over thirteen, but under sixteen. Somehow, I was walking down the main strip with a couple of girls my age. I must have met them through neighbors of the beach house we were staying in. I wanted to hang out with them, so I think I told my family I was going for a walk or something. The girls had told me there was a party we could go to. I was so intrigued, as I had never been to a real party before. We arrived at the party, and I remember everyone there being much older than me. I remember someone giving me a beer, and then another beer, and another beer. I had never had alcohol before, so I quickly lost track of what was happening. I don't remember where my new friends went, but I do remember ending up being in a bedroom and there being guys in there. The lights were turned off, and I was being undressed. I remember being on my back and seeing different faces over me. I know there was a lot of laughing, so they must have been having fun. The next thing I remember, I felt sick. I opened my eyes and saw that it was light out. I could feel pain between my legs, and as I reached down to touch, I could feel that I was terribly swollen, and I winced at my own touch. I rolled over and saw that there was no one else in the bed with me. I pulled the sheet around my naked body, and made my way slowly to the bedroom door, calling out, "Hello?" as I opened the door. There was no one else there. In fact there was no one in the entire house at all.

I felt like I had to pee as well as vomit, so I found the bathroom, and as I sat on the toilet gingerly, I began to cry in pain as I urinated. It stung so badly. I grabbed the waste basket at the same time and puked into it. I was sick and dizzy and had no idea where I was. I'm not sure how long I sat there, but I eventually went back to the room I had woken up in and found my clothes. After getting dressed, I made my way out of the house and to the street. I walked to the main road and walked down the street, stopping to throw up as I went. I kept asking people where the police station was and after some time, I found my way there. I went inside and told the person behind the glass, "I think I was raped." They brought me inside, and I don't know why, but I told them that I had actually woken up on the beach. That someone had left me on the beach, and I had woken up there. I had told them about the house and the party. An exam was done on me, and it hurt so bad, I almost couldn't bear it. I did not feel like anyone believed anything I was saying. The entire time I felt as if I had done something wrong. The police wanted to know where the house was located, and I showed them exactly where it was. For some reason, I actually remembered that the house was on O Street right off the main road, but I don't think they found anyone there. I remember my family coming to get me, and I remember everyone being really annoyed with me. They took me home, and I went up to my room and slept. When I got up, it may have been that day or the next, but I had wrapped myself in a blanket and was sitting on the side porch with my knees up against my chest, resting my head on them. I remember hearing my father making the comment that someone who has been raped does not want to go sit outside on the porch. My heart sank just then. That was when I knew that no one believed anything I had said. The fact that a bunch of guys had sex with their daughter was more of an embarrassment than it was a violation of my body. The humiliation I was feeling meant nothing. I was to recover from this alone, and deal with it the only way I knew how and that was to blank it out, and pretend nothing had ever happened. We left the beach that summer and that was it.

There were never any follow-up questions by the police for me, as far as I know. I don't believe there was even an investigation into what happened to me that night. I don't remember ever going to court, or having someone fight for me. It makes me sad, because I am realizing that I am that girl who I have seen countless times. The girl whose traumatic experience has been swept under the rug, because it's too much to handle for the ones who are supposed to fight and speak up for her.

I learned to fight for myself eventually, but that wasn't until many years later. After this, I became promiscuous, not caring what anyone thought of me. More than ever I needed something to make my pain go away. There were tons of parties in my town, and I attended as many of them as I could. Always telling my parents I was going to a friend's house. I would get drunk and let guys that I didn't even know or like have sex with me. They were always older than me, and I know they didn't care how old I was. I didn't care what was happening to me. I would wake up on the floor, in bed next to someone, or alone in someone's bed wondering who I had been with. Feeling ashamed and worthless, I would make my way home. My parents must have worried about where I had been when I came stumbling into the house the next morning, after being missing all night. I didn't care what they said to me, and I wasn't afraid to show it. I was angry, and for good reason. It came out in rebellious behavior and issues in school and at home. I walked out of school all the time. I would go to friend's houses, or just to walk around. I hated my life at home, and showed my parents by swearing at them, and refusing to do anything they said.

The impact of the sexual abuse I experienced was life changing. I began to react in the most negative of ways. I felt different about my existence now. I began to disconnect and retreat into the safer places my mind created for me. I couldn't trust now, and it showed. My behaviors were changing drastically. My parents were frustrated and didn't understand or know how to help me. They weren't privy to the mixture of unwanted thoughts and feelings these events had caused.

As I said before, we were a churchgoing and very religious family, so to them, the only way to quiet my demons was to turn to the church. The consensus was that I was inhabited by an evil spirit. That's right, I was possessed. Clearly that must be it! Well, the next step was—that's right, you guessed it—an exorcism. An attempt to free me, the possessed one, of the spirit that had somehow taken over my body. My God, it was true, I really was to blame for the feelings I was having. I already felt like I was damaged goods. I hated to look at my own body, because I felt disgusting. My poor young mind was now convinced that it was my fault.

The event was to take place at our home. I dreaded it, but had to comply. Our pastor, who is also my godfather, came over to perform the act. I did love him very much, and trusted him, but what he was doing upset me very much. He asked me if I knew what was happening. (Yes, I was being blamed for becoming a crazy sexual abuse victim, and I want you to leave me alone) I sat on the living room couch, and he began to pray and then speak to the spirit inside me. I don't think it could hear him. I wanted out of that house so badly. I felt so small, so alone. The room just got smaller and smaller, and I folded my arms across my chest to protect myself from the feeling. I felt angry and embarrassed that this was happening. Why couldn't they just let me go up to my room and be left alone? Why wouldn't everyone just leave me alone?

They began "praying in tongues," which is a religious term they used for being so deep in the Holy Spirit that you are speaking a language only God can understand. I was used to hearing this, because it was a regular occurrence at our church. It always seemed awkward to me when I heard people speaking this way, but I didn't think too much of it, because I was raised to believe in it. But this night was different. It was being used on me, and I hated it. I hated everything about it; the sound of it was driving me nuts, and all I wanted was for them to stop. It didn't stop; it just continued, and my parents participated in it trying to cast the demon out of my body. After what seemed like an eternity, everyone became frustrated with me, saying I wasn't cooperating. That's right, because this was ridiculous to me, and it was making me feel unwanted and even more like I had done something wrong. This wasn't helping me at all. I wasn't writhing around on the floor; my body wasn't contorting or twisting in any way. They wanted me to pray over myself and say things to the evil presence that they were convinced was in me. I didn't understand why I had to do anything. I began to cry, and soon I became angry and refused to participate. Due to my refusal, the exorcism was ended, and I was finally allowed to leave the room. I hated all of them for doing this to me. I hated all of them for making me feel this way. After all, it wasn't a demon from Hell that had made me behave the way I did; it was a devil here on Earth who had destroyed my view of the world and of myself.

3

JUMPING JERKS

Before turning to the drugs, I actually thought I had a mostly normal life. I had a good family; I had friends. My best friend was Mercedes. I loved Mercedes. We had a bond that I hope my daughters will have with their friends. We were recently reunited after not seeing each other for twenty years, and when we saw each other, it was as if not even a day had passed.

We did, of course, get into some trouble together. In fact, when as an adult I told my father that I had reconnected with her, he jokingly said, "I don't want you hanging out with her!"

I had a guy friend when I was younger, a guy who played football. We were friends and nothing else. His mother used to call me "hourglass." Those were the days when my body was still perfect no matter what I ate. Boy, are those days so over.

Now Mercedes and I had always heard about his crazy ex-girlfriend. I had heard she wanted to "kick our asses." I guess she was jealous of our friendship.

We would always tell our parents that we were going one place, and we were actually going to another. One night, I went to visit our guy friend, and I think we were getting ready to go out. We were just hanging out at his house when someone called my name and said I was wanted outside. I stepped out, and some girls came running up the stoop stairs, from the left and the right, and they started hitting me. I fought back the best I could, but at that time I was young and had never been in a fight; I was defenseless.

As I got older and fell deeper into the life, I became a fighter. I would fight anyone, girl or guy. It didn't matter; they were gonna get it. I had a lot of anger, and I was not afraid. I believe I am still that way, but I channel it differently. I hope I use it for good. (OK, laugh if you want.)

But on this night, I was no fighter. I was outnumbered. I was just a kid who had been hanging out with her friend.

They had me down on the ground and one of the girls was yelling, "F— up her face. F— up her face."

Her cohorts obeyed and began kicking me in the face. Despite my efforts to protect myself, a couple of those kicks hit their mark. One got me good right in the eye and cut me. I still have a scar in the corner of that eye.

I remember finding my friend Mercedes. She was cleaning the blood off of my face for some time after it was over. It hurt so badly, I cried. I was so frightened. I had never been beaten up before, and frankly, it sucked.

But the physical wounds eventually healed, and I continued with my life. This was what I call a small trauma. Those are the ones that I don't think of too often and even when I do, they don't have a heavy impact. The other traumas are bigger; they run through my head often, sometimes every day for months at a time. They have molded my thinking and caused me to create a "bubble life" where I can control (or once thought I could) what happens there. Boy was I mistaken!

4

WHILE YOU WERE SLEEPING

Once again, a predator would arrive to use me and be on his way. What is it about sexual predators that they are so cowardly? They creep in while you are sleeping and attack.

Even after I moved out at seventeen, my parents always let me come home. Well, in the beginning they did. I was still very young and had come to stay at their house. They eventually got sick of my shit, but in the early years, they always wanted me to come home. No matter what I had been doing or where I had been, or what pain I had caused them, they always opened their doors to me.

One day, I was so exhausted from the lifestyle I had been living, that I lay down on the couch in the living room to take a nap. There was another needy, wandering soul from our church who had been staying in the spare room. He had been around our church for a long time. He had always seemed a little creepy, but he had never bothered me. What woke me was the phone ringing. I opened my eyes and saw him standing behind the island in the kitchen looking at me. I stood up to get the phone and walked toward him; he said, "Don't get up, I'll get it."

I went over anyway, it was only a couple of steps, and when I got to the other side of the island, he was covering himself up. I saw that he had a full erection underneath his shorts. He had been masturbating in the kitchen while he watched me sleep. I never told anyone, but when I think about it, I want to scrape myself with sandpaper to clean off the memory. What a pig!

It was another one of those moments when I was in shock and couldn't say a thing. The phone call was for me. It was my friend Mercedes. I don't remember what we talked about, but I couldn't even bring myself to tell her. He must have gone into his room or something. I can't even remember what happened afterward. I must have blocked it out. More parts of my life had been taken from me without my permission.

It really makes me shake my head that there are so many people who hang around churches and families and do these disgusting things. The parents never know. But isn't there some sort of warning signal? Do these guys stare at the children too much? Do they try to get close to them all the time? Why doesn't anyone notice these perverts? They must have strange behaviors. They must give the adults a reason to be on guard around them. It can't be just me who gets that weird feeling about certain creepy guys who should never be alone with children. They weasel their way into families and make people feel bad for them. The whole time they are ruining the kids. I hate them.

That experience with the man who was pleasuring himself while watching me sleep is what I like to call another cold case. It's something that I never told anyone. It's also a case where the predator will never be brought to justice. I'm quite sure that the men who molested me are still walking around touching, watching, and destroying the lives of innocents. Making a dent in a young kid's psyche forever for a few moments of their own pleasure.

Who the hell did he think he was? If I could go back to that time with the courage and experience I have now, I would kick him in the face. I would definitely tell my dad.

I know my dad would have done something if he had known. Why didn't I tell him? Why is it so hard for victims to speak? What are we afraid of? I think the violation comes as such a surprise that we go immediately into shock. Especially children. We find it hard to believe that someone would do this kind of thing to us.

When these things happened to me, I was in shock. Afterward, the more I thought about what had happened, the more paralyzed I became. I don't ever remember feeling like I did something to deserve being molested. But I did feel humiliated. It all felt so gross.

The perps must know. They must know that you won't say anything. They rely on it. How do they know? How many others have they done this to? I would love to put together a list of victims and go do some lifetime damage to them.

5

THE GIRL UNDER THE STAIRS

During my later teen years my feeling of being uncomfortable in my own skin had become so intense, I was behaving irrationally most of the time. I ditched school and never did any of my work. I was emotionally all over the place, and my parents had no idea why, since I hadn't told them about me being molested. They tried everything to reel me in, but it was of no use. I searched for satisfaction with attention from men, but never found it. I began running away in the hopes that something would quiet the ache I felt.

I began staying in Brockton at different people's houses. I eventually ended up meeting the father of my first child. I was seventeen. We'll call him Rocky.

Yes, like the boxer—because I'm sure he thinks he's a badass, and he liked to throw punches. I was staying with someone I thought was a friend (who later ended up betraying me).

I was walking down the street, and a car pulled up next to me. Rocky was in the car staring at me. He started that stupid sweet-talking that guys do when they're on the prowl. He told me then that he was much younger than he really was. I think he was twenty-nine years old at the time. We started talking and days later I ended up going to his house, which was about a half an hour away from where I was staying.

We instantly began a relationship. I just went with it. I guess I was searching for something to fix me. A new home, a place with no triggering memories, or maybe I just wanted to be someone else. Not knowing what I was getting myself into, I started staying with Rocky. In the beginning, I went back and forth between his house and my so-called friend's house. I continued my partying until drinking made me vomit, and I began to suspect that I was pregnant. His baby would surely make everything better. I went to see Rocky and shared my news with him. He wanted me to stay with him all the time now that I was carrying his child, although he did question if the baby was his throughout my pregnancy. He soon became overly possessive, and started being violent.

He would choke me. One night we were fighting and he punched me so hard in the temple that I think I passed out for a minute. When I came to, I had a huge black-and-blue lump there. He could have killed me with that blow. He threatened me. He once held a twelve-gauge shotgun to my leg and said that if I ever cheated on him, he would blow my leg off. I was terrified, but I stayed. I wish that back then I had been able to leave before the horror began, but I didn't know how. I had never been taught how to leave an abusive relationship. Even if I had, would I have been able to? I don't know.

As I write this, I am biting gently on a lump of scar tissue left by a blow to the mouth that split my top lip into two pieces. I begged him to let me go to the hospital for hours. He only agreed to let me go if I stuck to his made-up story that a bunch of girls had jumped me. I promised to tell the doctors *his* story so that I would be allowed to seek medical treatment. He had his nephew drive me to the emergency room. I told my lies, and someone from plastic surgery came down and stitched my mouth back together. I was lucky; he was an amazing doctor. You can only tell that something happened to me if you look closely underneath my lip and see the scars. Of course I know it happened even without looking.

We lived in a basement apartment with no separating doors, just walled off rooms with hanging sheets. There was a shower unit and toilet at the far end of the basement. It had a dirt floor. I remember cooking down there, so there must have been some sort of kitchen. It was dirty and smelled like mildew. There was all kinds of junk scattered everywhere.

Here I learned how to cower. How to shrink. I should have been experiencing teenage love and high school drama; instead, I was being beaten into submission like an abused pet. My spirit was being crushed every day. While my friends were choosing their careers, I was trying to figure out how to keep my face and body free of blood and bruises.

Rocky used to take off to New York for days at a time. At least that's what I was told he was doing. He usually locked me in the basement before he left. Why? Maybe I had threatened to leave. I can't remember. The first time he did this, I tried to follow him up the stairs and out the door. He told me to stay downstairs, I kept grabbing him, and finally he pushed me just hard enough to send me backward down the staircase. He slammed the door shut, and I heard the lock clicking shut. I sat at the bottom of the stairs collecting my thoughts, crying because I was in pain physically and emotionally. I was feeling so small and helpless.

I collapsed onto the bed. I don't know how long I slept, but when I woke up I went up the stairs and tried the door, still locked. I could tell by looking at the basement windows that it was dark. I was hungry, but there wasn't any food. I climbed the stairs again and began banging on the door. I could hear voices from the first floor where one of his sisters and her family lived. Someone came to the door, and I begged them to open it. They didn't have the key. Well, that meant there was a padlock.

His family had to have known what had been happening to me because they all lived in a three-decker house; Rocky and I lived in the basement. They heard, they knew, and no one stopped him. Well, once his sister had told him she would beat him up if he kept beating me. That was nice, I suppose, but he kept doing it anyway.

I slept and waited, then waited some more. I think it might have been the next afternoon or evening when I heard someone calling my name. I jumped up and ran up the stairs to the door. "Yes, yes! I'm down here. Please let me out."

It was Rocky's nephew. He told me to calm down because he was going to open the door, but was not going to let me out. *What?* He said he had come to bring me food, but he was not going to open the door until I went down to the bottom of the stairs.

"No!" I said. "Please let me out! I won't say anything!"

I pleaded with him, but he told me that his instructions were to bring me food and not to talk to me or let me out. He said if I tried to leave and his uncle found out, I should know what would happen. Yes, I knew. Black eyes, chipped teeth, split lips, hands duct-taped while he punched me so I couldn't defend myself. Yes, all of these things had happened at Rocky's hand. So...I complied. I retreated to the bottom of the stairs. I must have looked like a pathetic wounded animal. The nephew unlocked the door and put down a plate of food. He looked at me, said, "I'm sorry," and closed the door.

I ate that plate of West Indian rice, beans, and chicken like it was my last meal, and then I slept again. When I awoke I started banging on the basement windows and asking someone, anyone, to let me out. Why didn't they come? Was everyone afraid of Rocky?

Finally, someone came and I heard the door being unlocked. I went up the stairs, and then—strangely enough, I couldn't bring myself to go outside. I went back down the stairs and waited for Rocky to come home. Now I understood how an animal, after being caged for a long time, will be afraid to venture out even when the cage door is opened.

As strange as it may sound to you, being locked up was not a surprise. After all, he had been beating me bloody on a regular basis. He beat me for even looking at another guy or for talking back to him. It seemed like the more I protested his treatment of me, the more beatings there were. He was especially angry if he thought I was lying about something. He accused me of that all the time.

All I wanted was a nice guy who cared for me and treated me nicely. I didn't want to be hit for having an opinion. It wasn't my dream to have my face smashed into the floor and screamed at. I needed love. I deserved it. Didn't every girl? Didn't I?

He didn't allow me to see any of my friends. Eventually I became completely isolated from everyone in my life. He then introduced me to a girl with whom I was allowed to hang out. He had been driving this girl to escort calls. I knew about her; sometimes I would call him when he didn't come home, and he would be there at her house or her friend's house. Friend? I think she was a coworker, not a friend. But I couldn't say anything like that. I was never allowed to question Rocky's doings. If I did, I always ended up bruised, bleeding, or both.

It was that girl who took me to a bar, pulled me into the bathroom, and gave me one of my first lines of cocaine. It was a welcome relief from the pain of the abuse I was experiencing. The mixture of the fancy drinks and the drug was liberating. I was intoxicated, but more than that, I was flying free for a moment in time.

It seems like this was his plan all along. Find a young girl. Break her down to nothing, then introduce her to people who live in a world of drugs and prostitution.

This sounds like a pimp's M.O., but Rocky never tried to traffic me. Perhaps it was an attempt to get me addicted so that I would lose custody of my son. Or, it could just have been an attempt to control me, to keep me in line. "Keep me in line." That makes me laugh now. Maybe he was just an asshole, who knows. There may not have even been a plan, but I believe there was something. He told me, "You can leave, but you will not take my son with you." I kept trying to leave, but someone was always there, watching, reporting back to Rocky. When I left with my boy, Rocky would find me. I was so screwed up in the head that I would go back.

Eventually I couldn't take the abuse any longer. I escaped from my abuser, but without my son. I called my father secretly and asked him to meet me at a store a couple of miles down the road. The drive would take nearly an hour, so I had to time my departure carefully. I told Rocky I was going to the store, and he gave me a time limit. I promised to come back within the time allowed, but I did not go back. I never would.

After I left Rocky, I didn't stay at my parents' house for long. I ran away again and ended up hiding at my friend's house. It was maybe an hour away from the basement I had shared with Rocky. This friend and I were getting ready to go out and she went outside for a minute. I looked out the window and saw a car pull up. She walked up to the car window, and the person inside handed her something, which I supposed was drugs, the usual thing. She came back up and said her friend wanted to talk to me. I figured I might get something out of it, and I trusted her, so I went outside and walked toward the car. As I got close, I realized that Rocky, my ex, was in the backseat.

I started to back away but he said, "Get in the car I only want to talk."

I was such a dummy. I was standing close enough to the car that he was able to grab my hand and pull me into the car. He told me to keep my mouth shut, or he was going to kill all my friends. He yelled out the window that if anyone in my friend's house said anything to anyone he was going to shoot all of them. I knew he had access to guns because he had once held a shotgun to my leg and said he would blow my leg off.

He told the driver, "You know what to do." They took off with me in the car. He immediately began punching me while he held my hair in his clenched fist. He kept asking who I was fucking and punching me in the stomach saying that if there was a baby in there he was going to kill it. He told me they were going to shoot me and dump my body somewhere. I knew this was true. He continued to beat me, and I fought back, knowing this was it; I was going to die. I began to pray, "Please, God, spare my life." Just then, I heard sirens. We were being pulled over!

He hissed in my ear, "When that cop comes over here you tell him we are just having a disagreement or you will never see your son again. Do you understand?"

I nodded.

I could see out of the corner of my eye that the officer was getting closer to the car. I thought to myself, if you want to live, you have to make a move. Don't be afraid, just go. As soon as he got to the car he asked what was going on. I unlocked the door and yelled, "He's trying to kill me!"

I scrambled out of the car and ran behind the police cruiser. I cowered there, sobbing hysterically. More cruisers came, and Rocky and the driver were arrested. The police found a gun in the car, and I was safe for the time being.

I heard lots of commotion, so I peeked out from behind the cruiser; Rocky looked at me and said, "You want to f— me? You want to f— me? I am going to f— you."

I knew what that meant. I wouldn't see my son. Rocky would do everything in his power to keep me away from him. And he did. He used a notarized statement I had signed, under duress, to win custody.

While we were living in the basement, Rocky showed me some sort of legal paper that said I no longer wanted custody of my son and agreed to give him to his father. He demanded that I sign it, but no matter how often he insisted, I always refused. Eventually, Rocky got so angry that one night he beat me until I gave in and signed the paper. Rocky said he had a notary friend who made it look legal.

He later brought that signed paper to court and claimed that I had given him custody. He said that I was a drug addict who had no business taking care of a child, and knew it. It breaks my heart to have to say this, but the time of our court date, I *was* heavily into drugs and alcohol. I had not seen my son for some time.

The judge asked me why I signed that paper. I told the judge that my ex abused me regularly and beat me until I signed that paper. The judge asked if I had ever reported the beatings to the police and I said no. Rocky laughed and said, "If I had beat her like that, don't you think she would have called the police or something? Or someone would have heard or seen something?"

The judge agreed. I had no money, no lawyer, and no credibility, so I lost my beautiful boy.

The pain of losing my son was unbearable. It drove me over the edge and I didn't look back for a long time. I was not in my rational mind. I could not have been rational. Reason had been beaten out of me, and I covered my wounds with chemical bandages.

6

GOOD-BYE, MY BOY

I was crashing, after days of running the street with no sleep. I have no idea how long I had been going like that.

I remember what triggered my breakdown. I had called to speak to my son (amazing that I could remember the number, when my mind was mush with drugs), and his father and his girlfriend at the time told me that I would never see my son again. Hearing this sent me spinning.

I understood that they didn't want to let a drug addict near a vulnerable child. Yes, but I believed that I was a drug addict because of what Rocky had done to me. The beatings, the degradation: they were too much. How did I end up the bad guy?

I couldn't handle these thoughts or the way they made me feel. I screamed into the phone, and they hung up on me. I walked over to a wall, stood in front of it, and smashed my head into it as hard as I could. It felt like slow motion. My head bounced back and my body followed. I was out before I hit the ground. Yup, I had knocked myself out—which, considering that I had been knocked out before, wasn't really a big deal.

I woke up in a bedroom. The friends whose house it was must have laid me down to rest. My head was pounding, and as I reached up to touch my forehead, I winced. I could feel a huge bump there that hurt to the touch. Everyone was quiet, probably sleeping.

My own anger had done this to me. Once again I felt the all-consuming emotional pain that comes when there is no more alcohol and no more drugs. Once again I was left with the emptiness and guilt of a lifetime. My using, my drinking, and my choices had created this madness. So why couldn't I stop? I couldn't control myself. I wanted these feelings to go away, because they were killing me.

I went into the bathroom and opened the cabinet. There was a box of razor blades there, brand new ones. I opened the box and took one out. It was so shiny. I stared at it, mesmerized. I went out into the living room and placed the blade against my skin. I made one small cut, but it barely put a dent in what I was feeling. I needed more. With one quick motion, I cut straight down my arm, from about the middle of my forearm to my wrist. My skin opened up and I could see that I had nicked the tendon. It was yellow. All I could do was stare. There was less blood than I thought there should be—or perhaps time stood still for a moment. Who knows? I must have yelled as I cut because my friend came in and yelled at me.

"No!"

Someone took me to the hospital. I actually remember the ride. He was driving like a bat out of hell, leaning on the horn to get everyone out of the way. He got me to the hospital in time. The staff asked me what seemed like thousands of questions. I think I got twelve to fifteen stitches on the outside of my arm, and some inside. (As I write this, I am trying to count the scars on my left arm.)

I was admitted to the psychiatric unit of the hospital. It was torture being locked up there. I tried once to escape when someone was leaving the floor in the elevator. I was tackled, given a shot of something, and woke up in a room, alone, in four-point restraints. That sucked. My next try was more successful. I waited until I got outdoor privileges. Once outside, I stared at the fence, trying to gauge whether or not I could make the climb with stitches in my arm. I made my way slowly toward the fence. Staff began calling out to me.

"Sarah, what are you doing?"

I ignored them. When I got close enough, I reached up with one hand, then a leg, one after the other and before anyone could do anything about it, I was up and over and running down the street.

The need to run, to move, to fill the void, was uncontrollable. It moved my body without my permission.

I was like a zombie, broken and bloodied, but moving just the same. Where was I going? What was the goal? Relief. To feel better, to numb everything. I found a friend who was holding and I started doing drugs all over again. As if nothing bad had ever happened to me because of drugs.

I still feel that urge at times. Sometimes I want to be numb. Unable to feel any of this pain. It still hurts, you know. I still cry and feel sick to my stomach when I think about some of what happened to me.

7

CLOSE CALL

I'm telling this part of my story because for most people this would be a traumatizing thing to witness. I'm sure it must have affected me, but at the time, it seemed normal.

I was lost in the drug world by this time. I had been living on the streets. This building was one of those dilapidated structures inhabited by drug addicts and dealers. The entrances were littered with empty nip bottles (one-shot liquor bottles) and dirty, broken syringes. The hallway reeked of urine and cigarette smoke.

I spent a lot of time in one of the second-floor apartments with people that I called friends. Forming bonds with people was a much different process in the street, although I have met some people in the real world who have the same morals as those from my past. I met people based on what they sold for drugs, what drugs they used, or what they could give me. Everyone wanted something in return, and I learned that quickly. Sometimes I gave and got nothing. I gave my body, my soul, and my dignity to that life. I am so amazed that I have anything left. Sometimes I got more than I had bargained for in the form of fights, bloody lips, black eyes, or being left out in the street with no place to sleep. It's a ruthless existence that no one should have to experience. I would seek refuge there between ducking out to get high.

One particular night I was in the apartment with the usual suspects. The guy who rented the apartment went out to buy something for us. He was taking forever to get back.

We heard a faint knocking and scratching at the door. One of the girls went to open the door, and I heard her from the hall.

"Oh, my God."

I turned my head and saw our friend who, when he left, had been wearing a white shirt and had light brown skin. What I saw now was a man in a red shirt with gray skin. He was holding his neck, and I could see blood trickling out between his fingers. He collapsed in the chair, and when he pulled his hand away, I saw his skin open up. There was a six-inch-long cut down his neck. Blood was spurting out of the cut. I fumbled to close the open wound with my hands. My fingers were slipping because of the blood. I was used to blood by then. Mine and that of others.

I was screaming, "Call 911!"

I held the cut together with my hands until the EMTs came. It was one of the more memorable moments of my life in that world.

I learned later that he'd been approached by some guys with a machete. When he wouldn't give up the money, they cut his throat. He had walked all the way back to the house.

When he got back from the hospital (of course he left against medical advice—that's what we always did), he had staples down the side of his neck. He walked in and handed me the money I had given him for drugs. That sticks in my mind. He almost lost his life for that money.

For years after that, whenever he saw me he would hug me and tell everyone, "This girl saved my life."

8

STICKS AND STONES, BREAK MY BONES

I was screaming; he was screaming. His eyes were bulging and spit was flying out of his mouth. I wanted to leave and he wouldn't let me. He was not my boyfriend—he was a dealer. He was in charge of the crack house where I crashed. There wasn't always a crash spot for me, but most of the time they let me stay. I would work the door from time to time and get packages for doing it. I began staying there on a regular basis. What a sick life we lived in that house!

Why were we screaming? I badly wanted to go out and get a drink, but his bosses had instructed the dealer to keep me from leaving. They did that from time to time to remind me who was in control. I knew there would be a fight if I tried to leave, but I needed the drink so badly that I was willing to put myself in danger for it.

I kept running for the door, and the dealer kept pushing me down. I was not giving up. I felt like a caged, abused animal fighting for freedom. He grabbed me, pushed my head into the couch, and drilled his fist into the side of my face. I heard and felt the bones crush. The pain was unbelievable. It was blinding.

The entire left side of my face swelled up. I badly needed to go to a hospital. I was begging, but he would not let me go. The men who ran this house were afraid that I would tell the police.

(I know now that he had broken my cheekbone. There is an obvious indentation in my face.)

After what seemed like an eternity, he finally let me go downstairs to the first-floor apartment where one of the other guys worked. How generous!

The first-floor guy was shocked. He kept saying, "Oh my God, oh my God!" He gave me ice to hold against my e, and he tried to get me to eat. I asked him to please let me out to go to the hospital, but he refused.

He let me lie down in his bed. So nice of him, right? I felt him lie down next to me, and I knew what was coming. He began touching me. Rubbing my back then pressing himself up against me. He wanted sex. Of course! Even though the entire side of my face was swollen and bruised, and I couldn't see out of my left eye. But that's the life, right?

The life had taken everything from me and then, when I thought I had been robbed of everything, it found more to take. Even when someone was nice to me, I knew he wanted something. I only knew men who took advantage of my pain and weakness.

It was episodes like this that made me develop a wall of protection. I needed it. I needed something to keep me safe, and all I had was me. It was always safer to just keep my guard up because in that world, they were all predators. It was every man for himself. Yes, I did have running partners, but I mostly had to fend for myself. As I did for many years after even after I got out of the life.

9

BACKBONE

I continued to wander through life aimlessly. I met someone else who I was sure would love me forever and take away the emptiness I had felt for so many years. We hooked up with each other and soon moved in together. We had a fun time in the beginning, but it soon changed to the familiar uncomfortable feeling I always got when it began to turn bad. He sold drugs, and I used them. I thought I was fooling him, taking hits of crack cocaine while I was supposed to be taking a bath, saying I was going to the store, and not coming back until days later. We had no sense of commitment, and we both cheated on each other on a regular basis, and neither one of us took care of our apartment. We destroyed our home and ourselves.

It had turned into another volatile relationship. We were fighting one night. He was in the house with a friend and a girl he was seeing on the side (as in, cheating). They were planning to go out, and I was saying he couldn't. We began arguing and then, as it always did, it got physical.

I was walking toward the front porch; suddenly, I sensed him behind me. I felt an impact, then the worst pain I had ever felt in my life. He had kicked me in my tailbone. I went down instantly. He said something like, "Good, now you can lie there and calm down."

Then they all left, and I was alone.

I don't know why the girl or the friend didn't call the ambulance for me. But that's how all the witnesses to my abuse were. They never called anyone or intervened. They always protected the offenders. It's sad but true that too many people do not care as much as you wish they would. I believe that is why I am such a strong advocate for my daughters. I was always alone in these abusive situations. I was threatened and told to keep quiet about what had happened to me. No one helped me. But I *will* tell, I *will* help, I *will* protect.

I tried to move but the slightest movement gave me a shooting pain in my lower spine. I began to cry, praying for God to take the pain away. I couldn't even roll over. I lay there for hours. I eventually fell asleep. When I woke up it was starting to get light out, and I still couldn't get up. I was, however able to slowly roll onto my back. My hip and shoulder hurt from lying on the hard floor all night. I eventually was able to get up. I'm not sure how long it took, and I don't even remember what happened once I did. But I'm here, so I obviously got up.

From this unhealthy union with another abusive man, something beautiful was produced. A beautiful baby girl. I conceived her during my drug use and continued using throughout my pregnancy. I hate what I did to her, but it's my truth. I must speak it. She was born addicted and had to live in the NICU for eight days. Every day I would go to see her. I wanted to nurse her, but for her protection, I had to pump my milk. The hospital would test it and give it to her if it was safe.

My parents stepped in and adopted her. They fell in love with her and did what I could not: raise her. My daughter and I are in contact with each other these days. She has grown into a beautiful, smart, successful woman and I love her.

10

DON'T LET THE DOOR HIT YOU

I met this one while I lived in the street. He had seen me before, and I knew he sold drugs. How romantic.

He basically gave me drugs for sex and called that a relationship. He felt bad for me, I guess. At least that's what he said. But they always said that. "You're such a nice girl, why are you doing this?" or my all-time favorite. "I could take care of you." Blah, blah, blah. I must have been tired of sleeping on smelly basement mattresses or walking the street all night so I moved into a rooming house with him.

I soon found out that I was pregnant. I did not stop using right away, and he didn't want me to run the street. He thought if he gave me all the cocaine, crack, and alcohol my habit needed, I would stay put. Wrong again. I took off all the time, and he would come find me and ruin my high. I was so pissed.

We eventually got an apartment right before Savvi was born. I did stop drinking and using at some point.

He was arrested when she was still so tiny. I think she was a couple of months old. He got three to five years in prison for selling drugs. He should have gotten more for feeding drugs to his unborn baby in an effort to control her mother, but I have to admit, I was also to blame. I would have found drugs elsewhere if he hadn't given them to me. I was the one putting them into my body. During the years that he was serving his sentence, I met someone else, and got pregnant by him, thinking that this would surely change my life for the better. There was no real relationship there at all. I gave birth to another baby girl. I nicknamed her Bug, because she just looked so tiny in her blanket. "Snug as a bug in a rug!"

When Savvi's father got out of jail about years later and wanted to see his daughter, I didn't have a problem with it. What I didn't like was that he was constantly asking me to get back with him again. I didn't want that.

At one point, I let him sleep on my couch for a couple days because he said he had no place else to go. Liar! On the third night, I woke up to him standing in my bedroom doorway in his underwear. I told him to get out. He kept begging. I tried to let him know that I meant business without waking my girls up.

He did this a couple of nights in a row. The next morning I needed to go shopping. Before leaving, I told him to be gone when I came back. Of course when I came back and opened the door he was still there. I put the girls in my bedroom. I picked up his jacket, opened the front door, and told him to leave. We started yelling at each other.

I said, "If you don't want to go back to jail, get out."

His eyes changed then. They glazed over and went from regular eyes to practically bulging out of his head. He slammed my door shut and started screaming in Spanish. "You want to send me back to jail?" He yelled this over and over. He was throwing punches by now. He pushed me onto the floor, jumped on my back, and started hitting the back and sides of my head. He was trying to punch me in the face, and I was protecting it with my arms. Then I heard a little voice. "No, don't, no!"

It was Savvi. She began hitting him. She was so small; she was perhaps five years old then. I raised my head to look at her. He flung out his arm, hitting her tiny body and throwing her across the room. While my face was still exposed he landed a punch that cracked my nose. Then, as quickly as it had started, it was over.

He grabbed his coat and tried to run out the door. I was on the phone calling 911 and trying to hold him in the house for the police. He got away, but the police caught him a few days later, and he was on his way back to jail.

I had to have closed reduction surgery on my nose. It seems like a minor physical injury, compared to some I had endured. What hurts my heart is that my girls heard the beating and one of them got hurt trying to save her mama. Savvi was brave even then. So maybe that's why now, no matter what happens, I will go to save her.

11

CASE CLOSED

I could not get out of this life no matter how many times I went to treatment. I had now given birth to four children by four different men. My son had stayed with his father, my second child was being raised by my parents, and my two youngest daughters were with me as I continued my constant bingeing and passing out all the while calling myself a mother.

I was living in an apartment with the girls. I had asked one of the neighbor's kids to stay with them while I "went to the store." Where I actually went was to the bar to get drunk, and to meet someone to buy drugs. I returned to my apartment after what I thought was a short period of time, when in fact, it was hours and hours later, and there were people outside waiting for me. My door was open and when I asked what was going on, one woman told me I needed to call the local police. When I asked her why, she replied, "Because that's where your children are." My heart sank. I knew I deserved this. I called the police station, and they directed me to call social services since the girls had been placed somewhere else for their own protection.

I continued to get as messed up as possible every night and every day. The absence of my children was so painful that I tried to drown the hurt, which just made things worse.

I would be so high and drunk that I would miss visitation appointments with them, or I would show up completely out of it. It breaks my heart to think of it now. Bug, with her tiny little pigtails, was so happy to see me. She would run to me with a big smile on her face. Savvi, on the other hand, didn't trust me.

I can't even imagine what it was like for them: torn from their mother, even if she was a disgrace of a mother. The disappointment they must have felt when I didn't show up. What a jerk!

One morning I had been without my daughters for about ten months. I had been on a hell of a binge. I had run out of everything and was crashing hard. This was always the time when all the guilt and self-hate set in. I would keep thinking what a piece of shit I was. What kind of mother loses her children and continues to use?

I knew I was doing wrong, and at that moment, the only choice that made sense was to cut myself again. I believe that I was punishing myself as everyone had punished me for so long. It must be what I deserved. I had done this so many times. Doing things that I *knew* would injure me, or damage me, but I didn't care. I needed the drugs, or the pain, to find relief from my churning mind.

I looked around for a razor. The one I had been using to scrape cocaine resin off a plate seemed too dull, so I chewed open a new blue razor. I jammed it into my wrist, and with one quick motion, I was bleeding again.

Then the phone rang. Of course I answered it; I might miss something! It was the drug counselor I had been seeing. I told her what I had done and either she or I called 911; I can't remember which of us did it. An ambulance showed up in time to get me to a hospital. I had been spared yet again. Why was that? Was it to be here on Earth when my daughters would desperately need me later? Maybe.

I remember lying in the hospital bed and looking at my hand that was so swollen that my fingers looked like sausages. I was in so much pain, both physical and emotional. I had no drugs or alcohol in my system, and I was defenseless against my spinning thoughts. Here it came. The flood gates opened and all the shame came crashing in at once. What had I had done to my children, myself, to others? Guilt and remorse would not leave me alone.

Yet, I still wanted to drink. How could this be possible? It's a relentless beast, the alcoholism, the addiction, whatever you like to call it. It will not stop even after everything you love has been destroyed. When your name is no longer being spoken at the dinner table, it keeps coming. When your children are no longer living in your house and cry for their mother every night because their foster mother doesn't feed them and all she does is yell at them. It keeps coming. It will not stop until you are DEAD.

"My God, please help me. Please take this from me, please let me live. I want to live." I pleaded with Him. He listened. I never had another drink or used another drug after that day.

Here's an interesting thing. I damaged the nerves in both of my hands when I cut them. While this latest injury was healing, I didn't know whether or not I would have full use of one of my hands. Not only did it heal, but I later became a massage therapist, using these two damaged hands, now turned healing hands, to help others. I still have numbness in my hand and pins and needles in almost all of my fingers. The scars are very noticeable and people ask me about them all the time. Maybe I'll tattoo over them!

12

ADDICTION STUFF

I do not like to dwell on the fun part of my life on the street, a time in the beginning when there were limos, parties, and lots of attention from men. Those things felt good. Being high and drunk felt good then. I floated so far away, I felt free. I felt invincible.

(I had already been drinking by the time I was sixteen; I started going deeper into drug use around the age of nineteen. By then I was fully into the life. Doing whatever I needed to do to "get right.")

No, what I need to remember is being cold while I was walking the street. No place to sleep, no food, no winter clothes to keep me warm. I remember one

Christmas morning when I was walking in the streets, alone and freezing my ass off. I was so cold, so hungry. There was just one straggler, one car that was prowling, one client. I thanked God for him. He meant warmth for me. He meant money to buy a bag of chips, but most importantly, he meant money for relief. Chemical relief from the disgust I felt for myself. Being high was the only time where I felt in control, important, even successful. Sad, isn't it?

After a short-lived high, I would crash. I would be disgusted by what I had done. I couldn't bear feeling so guilty and ashamed of myself. The only way I knew how to make that feeling go away was to get a nip (a shot of alcohol) or a pint, some powder to cook or powder already cooked up. The time between feeling the guilt and having my medicine was excruciating.

Here's a story I tell a lot. I had found myself walking around without any shoes. I can't to this day remember what happened to them. They weren't worth anything, so I know I didn't sell them! OK, maybe I did—who knows? I was filthy, so who would want to wear my shoes? Ew. Anyway, the skin on my toes and heels was splitting and bleeding. I was limping, but I needed to walk to get what my sickness told me I needed. That made sense to me then. A lot of crazy things made sense to me when I was in the life.

At the time, nothing seemed to phase me. What I mean is, nothing scared me into getting clean. The pleas from my family didn't work either. The monster had taken over, and I was its prisoner. So was anyone who came into my life and that includes the little ones born into my misery. I was a horrible mother who didn't take good care of my kids. I didn't even get to raise my two oldest kids, and I lost the youngest two to Social Services for ten months. I wasn't there for them because of the selfish life I was living. When I think about those times it hurts so badly.

I think people, myself included, forget that there are addicts who, in all their glorious messy splendor, are someone's son, mother, daughter, wife, grandmother/grandfather, etc. They have become someone else, but never actually commit the atrocities that we hear about in the news, or read about in books about people's lives. There are some who just get high, do what they can to survive and basically destroy themselves. They don't rob stores and kill the owner, they don't rape young girls. They just live their miserable existence until someday they can get it right, or sadly, and way too often, they die. Are addicts the only people who commit crimes? Absolutely not, but I do notice that once in court, addiction seems to be blamed for many things.

I myself have used it as a get-out-of-jail-free card, and gone straight to rehab instead of jail.

When I am alone, in my house, in my car, or at the gym with my music blasting, I think about what it is like for me now. It feels awful sometimes. To not be able to numb any of it. The pain, the anger, and frustration of everyday life, not to mention the extras that were added along the way. There are moments when I have to breathe in, then out, then in again over and over again, and even that doesn't ease the weight of what I have had to bear. It's supposed to help—well, that's what my therapist says—but it usually doesn't, and I'm left with my spinning head for hours on end. It takes a lot out of me just to feel these feelings without a buffer. Working out has been one way, but I can't work out all day long. I still wake up at night with intense fear, and I still check every door and window before bed.

Anyone who can stay away from a drink and a drug on a daily basis and still show up for life every day, after being dependent on them, is to be commended. It was hard as hell to go from living in basements to owning a business, but I did it. I think I have to remind myself sometimes where I was and how much I have been through, so I can see what I have actually accomplished.

At age thirty two, I had been able to get clean, but my life didn't suddenly become a bed of roses. I wanted to go back to school. I had already gotten my GED while I was still using (which was a shocker because I could barely put two thoughts together, let alone study). So, I ended up going to a school that taught massage therapy. I applied for student loans and an education grant. I was terrified when I started, because they told us that we would be taking anatomy, physiology, and other things that I never thought I would be able to understand. Someone who had just come out of eighteen years of street life couldn't possibly do this! I thought I was stupid; I was sure I would fail; I thought of withdrawing before I even started. This was the first time I had ventured out into the real world on my own. Without my crutch. Without my vices.

I found out something about myself: I had unstoppable drive. I could walk, take a bus, a train, and another bus—in a blizzard!—to get my education. I would show up at school with my feet soaked and freezing cold, but hungry to learn. I graduated on the Dean's List.

I was so proud. At the graduation ceremony, one of my daughters ran up on the stage to hug me. I was so moved. They were proud of their mom! This was an unforgettable moment for me. Instead of being embarrassed by a mother who stank of alcohol, who was always hung-over, puking in bathrooms, shaking on the floor…instead of a mother who missed birthdays, visits, events, even the early years of her children's lives, I had become someone they could admire.

Six months after graduating, I started my own massage therapy business. It started as one small room with three clients, the people I had practiced on during school. My business grew, and I moved into larger quarters in the center of town. I joined the Chamber of Commerce and attended events and fundraisers. I learned that I had a passion for massage, a talent for business, and a gift for talking to people.

Most of the time, my life was wonderful. There were times when my PTSD (Post Traumatic Stress Disorder) would rear its ugly head. I had to struggle with stress from being around men or being around too many people in one day. I fought through it. I had accomplished so much and felt that I was on top of the world. Then it happened….

13

SHE

She had never been late for curfew. Never really had any problems. At that time her grades had dipped, but I had chalked that up to middle school troubles. But that was not the problem. The problem was something else. That was the beginning of three years of pure nightmare.

I was waiting for her to come home. The clock showed nine, ten, eleven, and then twelve. At first I thought she was just testing me, but as time wore on, I knew something was wrong. My heart began to beat faster in my chest. I picked up the phone to call the police and tell them that my fourteen-year-old daughter had not come home. She had left the house earlier that day to meet a friend and had not returned.

My youngest was asleep in her room, so I couldn't go to the station and do the one thing I had never thought I would have to do: fill out a missing persons report for my child. The police said that they would send an officer to my house and asked me to have a recent picture of my daughter ready to give to the police.

My hands were shaking as I answered the door. I tried to talk quietly so I wouldn't wake my little one. The police called the parents of the friend she had gone to meet and confirmed that she was not there. My heart sank.

"God, please let her be OK," I prayed.

I began to feel a new fear, a fear that I had never before felt. Fear not for myself, but for my loved one. This fear would not leave me for the next three years. It was so overwhelming that I could barely process it. I felt as if I were scrambling for a place in my mind to put the fear, but finding that there was no more room. This felt worse than any trauma I had ever experienced. Nothing else could touch it. Where was she?

My youngest daughter would be up soon. How would I shield her from this? I would find out later that it was impossible to keep her from being impacted, but I had no idea how deeply it would shake her.

I began calling my closest friends as the sun was coming up. I remember Cali coming to take my daughter away, so that she wouldn't be around for whatever horrible thing might be coming. My friend Lala came to run interference for me and hold my hand through it all. I was crumbling.

The police came to search Savvi's room. Lala and I helped. We flipped mattresses and pulled out drawers, and made heartbreaking discoveries. We found expensive clothing that I had not purchased for her. Adult clothes. Things no fourteen-year-old girl would wear, things appropriate for places no fourteen-year-old girl should be. There was expensive makeup from Macy's. Too much for a little girl to afford. But nothing, absolutely nothing, not even my darkest night in the street could have prepared me for what I was about to find. I can't even remember where in the room it was, but it shook me to the core of my being.

It was the driver's license of a woman I knew. She was the wife of a registered sex offender who lived directly across the street from us. I had known her previously. She had married a man who had been charged with child rape, indecent assault, and battery on a child under fourteen. He had been convicted of the second charge.

My hand was shaking, and as I opened my mouth to speak, Lala saw the look on my face and asked, "What is that?"

I couldn't speak for what seemed an eternity. I somehow managed to squeak out, "This woman's husband is a child rapist."

People have asked me what went through my mind at that moment. I remember feeling heat that rose up from my belly, filled my chest and shoulders, then my throat and face. For a moment I was almost blind; I could only see shapes. My legs weakened, and I leaned forward, reaching for something to hold me up. I went down to my knees and collapsed on the trundle bed. It was hard to believe that this could be happening to me.

The local police assured me that they would find my daughter.

The waiting was unbearable. Later that day, after I had spent many hours of searching for her, putting posters up all over our town and the surrounding areas, she was found. She had contacted a friend. I went with the police detectives to find her near a pond in town. She was exhausted and crying. We immediately took her to the emergency room, and it was there that

I had my first introduction to the Human Trafficking Unit here in Boston.

A friend of hers had given local police some information about an older man who had been picking her up on different occasions. I do not want to harm an ongoing investigation, so I cannot give any more information on this man.

I would like to be able to say that the nightmare ended there, but it did not. She was to disappear over and over again. Each time, she would be gone longer and longer. The worst absence was a month and a half long.

I attempted to get her into therapy, but she refused. She became distant and refused to talk to anyone. I was trying everything I could to help her, but something evil had her in its grip. Whatever it was, it was stronger than she was at the time. She would never tell us where she had been.

I was to find out later that, during the time I felt that I was losing her, she was undergoing what the Human Trafficking Unit called grooming. They told me that the predators will try to drive a wedge between child and parent. They give children nice things and make them feel special, all the while planning to use them for their own gain or pleasure.

I had seen this sort of thing in movies, but never did I think I would experience it myself: putting my own child's picture up on The National Center for Missing and Exploited Children website. Once was tough, but having to do it more than that was excruciating.

All too often, I just couldn't take it any longer and ended up in a fetal position on my boyfriend Justice's couch. He was a big support then: he would make sure I kept my work schedule, remind me to pick up my youngest daughter from school, and invite me to his house for dinner—which he would cook. Bug, my youngest daughter, and I would sometimes stay at his house.

There were days that I couldn't even function. I was so angry, so afraid. I didn't know where my girl was, but I feared that the worst was happening to her. I felt so helpless waiting for…I don't know. I remember lying in my bed after she had been missing for a whole month. I had no energy, no hope, nothing but the expectation that I would never see her again.

When the phone rang, I always thought, *There it is.* I thought of it as The Call. The phone call where they tell you they have found a body that matches the description of your child, and they need you to come down and identify the body. I imagined going to the morgue. What it would be like, what it would smell like.

Would her face be mutilated? Would she have clothes on?

Sometimes I would open my eyes in the morning and immediately feel my head start to pound and tears run down my cheeks. I wanted to stay in bed and let my body regain its strength, but I couldn't. I had another child who was suffering, who was worried about what might have happened to her sister. I had a business to tend, one that was falling apart. So I would get up, shower, and move like a zombie though the day.

I don't know how I got through it. I imagined her being abused, perhaps being locked in a basement or an abandoned building, perhaps being smuggled out of the country. I imagined bruises and blood. I could hear her screaming. Perhaps she had died alone, or perhaps she had been strangled, stabbed, or beaten to death, and dumped in a shallow grave. I feared that I had lost my daughter, even though no body had been found. I often found myself praying, "God, help me. Please help. Please help me."

These dark thoughts were real for me because I knew that world. I knew what happened to those girls. I had heard. I had even known a girl who was beaten to death and her body left in the snow like a piece of shit. Because I knew that these things happened, they were real possibilities to me, more real than they were to anyone else. Well, maybe they were real possibilities to law enforcement. Police see such horrors all too often.

Sometimes I expected the worst *because* I had slipped free of evil's grasp. I knew how hard it had been. What were the odds that she would survive too?

Then I would veer into anger. I thought of what happened to child sex slaves, I thought of it happening to her, and I raged at the perpetrators. I wanted them to be found and punished. Not just my daughter's abusers, but all of them. Anger, rage, hate, revenge: they ruled me for a long time.

In the beginning, I had lots of support. Everyone wanted to be my friend; everyone asked me what was going on. Time dragged and my supposed friends went away. All except for a couple of women.

Kara was always a phone call away. She never abandoned me, even though she struggled with her own difficulties. She has truly been an amazing friend.

Lala, who was with me the first time Savvi went missing, was another true friend. She was always asking me if we needed to take a ride with a bat and a shovel.

I knew that some people were in contact with my daughter. I knew that they were lying to the police about her whereabouts. I knew their names, I knew where they lived, and I wanted to kick in some doors and crack some skulls. But I knew that wouldn't get justice for Savvi or any other abused girls. I had to let law enforcement handle this, so that they could bring the perpetrators to justice. I wanted all of them to get what they deserved. Besides, once they were in jail—well, you know what happens to anyone doing time for violating a child.

I had to tamp down my anger, so I would go to the gym to beat my thoughts into submission. I never actually gave into those angry urges. I had a business to run, and I needed to keep it together for my youngest daughter.

It was a long time before the nightmare was over. Savvi finally spoke up for herself. Arrests were finally made. David Manasian and Madonna Say were arrested and charged with trafficking my daughter. He pled guilty to trafficking her for sex, and his girlfriend, who cooperated with the US attorney's office by testifying against her boyfriend, pled guilty to misprision of a felony, which means she knew about and participated in a felony, but didn't report it.

It was about a year before they would be sentenced, and I would be able to see them in a courtroom. Was I out for revenge or justice? I still don't know. Revenge, I think would have been me acting on the feelings of anger outside of the judicial system. So while I thought the thoughts of revenge, I used the legal process to get it, but I still don't feel the relief that I thought I would. Is it because there are so many regulations in the legal system, that the sentences given were not enough as far as I was concerned? Or is it because my own traumas have left me with the feeling that only the extreme will do?

I know in my mind that revenge would land me in prison. Then who would care for Bug? She deserves to have her mother in her life to help her heal from all of this as well as her own stuff. I have envisioned many ways of taking out my revenge, but I leave it at that. Now that both sentencings are over and done with, there is a part of me that asks, Now what do we do? We have nothing now. Of course this isn't true, because there is much to do. Between self-healing, Bug's healing, thinking of her future and mine, as well as constant worrying about Savvi who is still struggling with her addiction, I can barely keep my head on. It feels like there is no recourse.

I had begun thinking about what I would say to Manasian the day my daughter told me what he did to her. I thought about it every day in one way or another until the sentencing was upon me. What I mean is, I don't think there has been a moment where it was not on my mind in some capacity. I had depended on him being arrested. I needed it. I craved it, even lived for it at times. She had showed me his picture via Facebook, the day she was recovered. When I saw his face, I was relieved that we now had someone to go after. It always feels better when there is someone to direct my anger at. A name, a face, an actual human being, as low a form as he may be. I loved that he was held without bail. I knew that there was a possibility that if he was released on bail, he could come after Savvi, or even me and Bug.

While Madonna Say was abused by Manasian, she still knew right from wrong. In my eyes, she didn't get enough of a punishment. I was severely abused, and never once did I ever think of selling a child. When

I was in the street, there were men who came around asking for younger girls or even boys; we told them to f— off. If there were even an underage girl that came around trying to get high with us, or make money, no one I knew would have anything to do with her. It was considered taboo to mess with a child. Even in a drug-induced stupor, I knew not to do it. Madonna wasn't even on any drugs! I hate that "My boyfriend made me do it" defense. I have been beaten bloody many times, and I would have taken the beating instead of doing something like that to a young girl. She only did two weeks in jail, and got out on bail. The judge sentenced her to one year probation with six months of that to hold a curfew, which could be changed, if she needed to work, or go to counseling. Oh, and the counseling was for her abuse by Manasian, not anything to do with her crime. She has even admitted that she wasn't sure whether or not she could stay away from Manasian. She did not have to register as a sex offender either. One thing that makes me happy is that she will never be allowed to vote. Considering what she helped to take from my daughter, I like that one of her rights was taken from her. I actually revel in it somewhat. Women should be able to vote as a right, and children should not be forced to sell their bodies. Take away my daughter's freedom and rights, you lose one of your rights. Seems fair to me. I have been called cold and even unfair in my thinking, because people think that I should understand her plight since I have experienced abuse myself. I do feel for women who are abused, but it all changes when they, in turn, hurt a child. There is an unspoken code that you NEVER sell a child, no matter what. I guess she didn't have to abide by that.

There are still pieces that may never be put together. That is one hard thing that I have had to come to terms with. Not knowing is the worst, but I have also learned when to leave a victim of abuse alone. When they are done talking, they are done. We still don't know how that woman's driver's license ended up in my girl's room. When the woman was questioned by police, she claimed to have lost it. Savvi says she found it on the sidewalk. The investigation into the woman and her child-abuser husband turned up nothing connecting them to my daughter. Do I think there is more to it? Probably. Maybe they got her high; maybe they were trying to get their claws into her. Or maybe it is nothing. Maybe Savvi did find it on the sidewalk, like she said. I wish I knew.

What I do know is she is an amazing, strong girl who overcame something terrible and stood up to people who could have taken her life. Through years of therapy, she has tried to turn herself around. She still struggles with her addiction, and I pray for the day she will be free of it.

14

BUG

Early on in Savvi's ordeal, I saw how it was affecting Bug. Her hair began to fall out. She was afraid of the dark again, as she had not been since she was little. She started biting her nails until they bled. Then she bit her knuckles. She would peel the skin off with her teeth. She absolutely refused to go to therapy.

After Savvi returned, things seemed to be going better for Bug. She had started hanging out with her friends again. She didn't seem afraid of the world any longer. Little did I know that Bug had slipped into a severe depression.

One day I found out she had been cutting herself. I was terrified. I took her for an emergency psychiatric evaluation, which revealed something terrible. Something that would destroy my life once again. My twelve-year-old princess wanted to take her own life! How can a child so young have thoughts about taking her own life? No, no, no.

She thinks about killing herself every day. Such words were actually coming from her mouth. Oh, God, please. I don't want this. God, please be with me; be with all of us.

I couldn't handle any more trouble, especially when I had just started to think that things were improving. Savvi was doing well. After twelve months of in-patient treatment she was being moved to an unlocked, community-based facility. I was just starting to breathe again. I just needed time to take a breath!

Then I found out what had really been happening. The kids at Bug's school were bullying her. I'm not kidding—these kids were brutal. She was being stalked by students on a social media site called Ask FM. They relentlessly called her fat. They called her a spic. They used racial slurs. They weren't just calling her fat and ugly. They were saying she was a whore and a slut. They accused her of multiple sexual acts. They urged her to kill herself and insisted that they wouldn't stop until the day she did. They threatened to hurt her when they saw her in school.

This wasn't just happening online. They were even writing these things on the bathroom walls. Her name, then "sucks dick." On sixteen different occasions, she had seen these things written about her in the girls' bathrooms.

Those kids knew what had happened to her older sister. They knew she had just lost her great-grandmother. Her first family death ever. (My first death since I became sober.) Bug was only twelve. She was a scared, vulnerable kid, and they were tormenting her. This had gone on for months.

Hearing these things made me sick to my stomach. It made the heat rise up from my belly and into my throat. But, believe it or not, this was not the worst. I was certainly not prepared for what I would hear next.

There were adults involved who knew what was happening and never once contacted me. These were educators whom I had entrusted with my child's well-being, and they were hiding this persecution from me. Despite her numerous attempts to get help from many different people in the administration, she was shunned. She was made to feel as if her plight didn't even matter. She had even been told by one of the teachers she had asked for help to wash the writing off the bathroom walls herself!

Which she did. Bug told me she bawled her eyes out the whole time she was cleaning it off.

What the hell was wrong with these people? Because of them, she had fallen into a deep state of depression. She felt hopeless and could only think of one way to end it. She was convinced that no one could help her. All those after-school TV messages say to tell someone, but when she did, they acted like it didn't matter. So why would she trust that any adults would help her?

She was immediately admitted to the hospital. I remember riding on the train, going to see her, and sitting in on some of her therapy sessions. She was in so much emotional pain that she started to disassociate when we talked to her about going back to her old school. Tears were pouring down her face. She told us that if she had to go back there, she would end up back in the hospital. The hospital was the only place she felt safe. She would miss her family if she had to stay in the hospital, but it was better than being bullied.

The little one whom I had sworn to protect from all the ugliness I had known. Despite all my efforts, she had been deeply affected by it.

It was so hard, going home from the hospital, feeling so empty. Knowing none of my children would be home. By this point I was numb. I do believe I had cried every tear I had. Are we allotted a certain amount? Maybe mothers get extra.

It would be a fight to get her into another school, but I was ready for a fight.

The clinicians had called the school about the abuse, and the school had responded by suggesting that Bug was making a bigger deal out of it all then it actually was. They also claimed that they only had one report in which she complained about bullying. Even more disgusting: a week after that phone call the principal of the school admitted, during a meeting I and the hospital had requested, that she did in fact know about the writing on the bathroom walls, as well as other instances of bullying, but that she had thought that the vice principal was handling the problem.

Now I had had dealings with this principal before, when Savvi went to that school. Savvi was being picked on pretty badly—not to the same extent as Bug, but enough to need some adult intervention. When the principal refused to do anything, saying there were no witnesses to the alleged bullying, I made a report at the police station. That prompted the principal to call a meeting between one of the girls (a bully) and her aunt, and me and my daughter. A week later, I got a text message from one of Savvi's friends, saying that Savvi was crying after being harassed again. I went to the school and told them about the text message. The school's first response? The school nurse demanded to know who had a phone and was texting me.

The principal came out of her office and called my daughter down. Savvi was crying hysterically and had broken out in hives. When she saw me, she collapsed into my arms. I glared at the principal. She turned to my daughter and said, "Savvi, didn't you tell me you had cramps earlier and that's really why you're crying?"

I was speechless.

But to get back to Bug's problems with the same woman—when I asked the principal why no one had called me, sent a letter, or even an e-mail when Bug was asking for help, the only explanation she could stutter out was that someone *must* have called me. Well, you can imagine how badly I wanted to hurt that woman. I couldn't believe what she was saying.

But that's not all. The story gets even better. Or rather, worse.

When we first arrived at the school for that meeting, Bug needed to use the bathroom. The principal offered to let her use the staff bathroom; she almost seemed to insist on it. But Bug wanted to go into the girls' bathroom and wanted me to go with her. The principal tried to get me to stay in the meeting room, but I said, no, I would go with her. As soon as we walked into the bathroom, my girl said, "Mom, look."

There it was. It said, "—— is a whore and…" The scrawl looked as if it hadn't been finished. Bug turned red and started to cry. I took a picture of it with my phone, for I suspected I would need a record later. We returned to the meeting room and I told the staff what we had seen. Everyone seemed shocked—except for the principal, who asked my daughter, "Why did you go in and use that bathroom? We offered to let you use the staff bathroom."

That was her only response to a child who was crying hysterically. Her own staff looked at her in amazement. This woman was unbelievable. Oh, and by the way, the guidance counselor and the teacher who had told Bug to wash the writings off herself, both of whom I had requested be at the meeting, didn't even bother to attend!

When I realized the principal wasn't going to take any action, I called the Board of Education as well as the state Office of Civil Rights. The OCR decided that there was enough reason to open a case, based on the sexual nature of the harassment Bug had faced as well as the racial slurs flung at her. The investigation is still pending, but I am told that it is close to a decision. Like I said, I am no pushover when it comes to my kids.

Bug came home after three weeks in the hospital. She lasted four days at home. She went to a local football game and was bullied there. She had a severe anxiety attack and was rushed to the hospital. While we were at the hospital, she had another attack. It looked like a stroke or seizure of some sort. She kept her right arm pinned to her side; her right hand was twitching, while her left hand came up by her mouth. She was making a horrible sound that sent chills through my whole body. I felt so helpless. The nurses came running, and after trying to bring her out of it, had to give Bug medication to relax the seizure.

This is what they did to my little girl with their cruel words and actions. My God, these people must be sick. How did they become so heartless?

This school, in my experience as well as the opinion of other parents I have spoken to, is notorious for hiding bullying. The principal has a habit of blaming the victim. They had always refused to do anything about it.

There is a new vice principal there now, who seems to have a grasp on what to do to keep the kids safe, but the principal…well, she, and others, need to account for their inaction in so many cases.

Bug made it through her second hospitalization, and she has been safe for a while now. Picking up the pieces of our lives will be difficult, but we will do it.

What I did to deal with the adults who were supposed to protect her is another story. I cannot discuss it at this time. It is enough to say that I dealt with that as I should have. I wish I could share more. But believe me when I tell you, I definitely did my job on that one!

15

THE GRAMMYS

Growing up, my grandmothers had been everything to me. There is something so wonderful about the special love I feel when I think about them.

In the beginning of my story, I mentioned being at my maternal grandmother's house in her upstairs closet. I also used to do that same thing in her basement. It was amazing to me how many things I would find down there. I didn't care that it was a basement at all. Dirty or not, I had exploring to do. There were endless boxes and bags to look through, and I was one curious little girl!

There weren't many things that excited me the way those times did, except dinner time. When they said it was time to eat, I made a beeline for the table. I usually got in trouble for eating too fast or not using my manners, but mostly for being fresh to my mother. My grandmother would look at me with huge eyes and bite the knuckle of her index finger. I knew this to be a warning that meant I had better smarten up.

I would sit in the living room with her while she played solitaire, watched television, and smoked her cigarettes. I ate as many snacks and bowls of ice cream as I could before getting yelled at. I remember when she quit smoking. I was so proud of her. I have always looked up to her because of that.

While I was in the deepest moments of my addiction, I didn't really see her. I was not, and for good reason, invited to family events such as holidays or birthday parties. It was several years into my recovery before I was invited back into the fold by my mother, who I know got the brunt of my torturous behavior. I remember the first time I went to a family event after getting clean. I believe it was Christmas at my aunt's house, and we were all sitting around the table. My father was saying grace, and as he began thanking God for making our family whole again, he started to cry. I hadn't seen him cry too many times, but he looked at me, and as I looked back at him, I cried too. The feeling of being with my family again was overwhelming. I had longed for it for so many years, and finally, here it was. I was with them again, getting hugs and kisses from the people I loved.

I continued on my journey with school and my two youngest daughters who had been returned to my custody not long after I got sober. One day I got a call that my grandmother had gone to the hospital for testing that revealed a brain tumor. There was to be a period of treatment, and my mother and aunt were taking care of her until it was time for her to leave us. The last time I went to see her, my mother told me if there was anything I needed to say to her, I should say it then. That made me so very sad because I knew it meant I would never see her again.

I sat on the chair by the edge of her bed and rested my head on the rail. Looking at her through teary eyes, I said, "Good-bye, Grammy. I love you."

That was it. I didn't see her again, but she is always in my mind as if she were still here with me. It was like taking a blow to the side of the head, something I knew a little bit about. There was a gasp, then a pause as my ears began to ring. The matriarch of our family who, in my mind, held most of the pieces of my childhood in her hands, was falling. It felt like my world was changing, again, without my say-so. I hadn't experienced a death in sobriety, and wasn't sure what it was supposed to feel like.

I attended her wake and funeral, not knowing what to expect of myself. The wake felt strange, and it hurt me to see her in the casket. She looked so tiny and not full of life like she was before. I already missed her terribly. Her funeral was hard, because I listened to my family members speak about her life and how wonderful she was. I felt guilty because I had missed so much of her life. At the reception after the funeral, my uncle gave a beautiful speech about how special she was to the family. He cried, which in turn made me cry. I cried for the years I had missed, and the time I had missed. I wanted it back, but that was not possible. So I keep the special memories that I do have and am grateful for the time that I had with her.

My dad's mother loved me with all her heart. Not only did I gain a father, but I had two grammys now, and what could possibly be better than that? She just loved everyone no matter how bad off they were; she knew there was good in them somewhere. I remember at around age seven, she would take me to church with her on Saturday nights, and I would fall asleep on her lap. She wouldn't let me fidget around and distract her from the service. She demanded respect in her own gentle way.

We had gone to church one weekend, and I was crying from pain in my mouth and was squirming around with my head in her lap. I had an abscess in one of my teeth, and I was in so much pain. That was the only thing that made me feel better, my Grammy. I ended up having the tooth pulled, but she comforted me, as she always did.

As I got older, and my behaviors changed from cute little girl to struggling teen, she was still there to comfort me. I wanted many times to tell her about the man who had molested me, but I could never bring myself to do it. It seemed impossible to tell such a terrible thing to someone so pure and good. So I kept it to myself and let myself get lost in the happiness I felt when I was with her. Forgetting that I had been violated, if even for a moment.

When I would relapse, she would ask me her usual questions: "How are you feeling? Are you ready to let God help you?"

I wanted so badly to be clean and make her happy, but I wasn't done, and nothing could change that until it was time. When I did finally get clean, she was right there to welcome me back with open arms. She would cry at the dinner prayer as my father thanked God for bringing me back to the world of the living. I cried too because my wish to make her happy had come true.

A few months before my tenth year in sobriety, she got sick. My father called me and said that he had been taking her to the doctor for pain she was having, but they couldn't figure out the cause. When he told me that, my worry set in. I always immediately begin to spin about any significant event. My heart races, and I think about the worst possible thing that could happen. I do this because my experience with horrible things happening has been the norm. I prepare myself for the worst because I am tired of being caught off guard. I think if I am ready, the blow won't be as much of a shock. Although he made it sound routine, I couldn't stop my usual way of thinking from occurring. He said that she was despairing because she felt that no one believed her about her pain. She had test after test and nothing was coming up.

I continued to deal with my everyday life, but I was always thinking about her, until my dad called me one day and told me that they had finally done a PET scan (A positron emission tomography is an imaging test that uses a radioactive substance called a tracer to look for disease in the body), and they found that she had lung cancer that had spread into her spine. They believed that it had originally spread from her colon. There it was again. That fear that grips so tightly. I was losing my last grandmother. Despite treatment, she would not live long. She passed within a few months. I was already numb and thought I couldn't feel much more pain, but her funeral was held in the church I had grown up in. I hadn't set foot in there for many years. I saw people who I hadn't seen in forever and it set off a string of emotions I was not prepared for. I sobbed uncontrollably during the entire service. Bug, now thirteen, was there with me, and she wiped my tears away as I, being her mother, had done for her so many times before. It was a bonding moment that I put away in my vault of special memories.

We went over to the cemetery, and as they lowered her into the ground, I was still crying and whispering to myself, "I'm not ready." I wasn't. I had too many bad things happen in my life, and she was one of the good things I had been blessed with. I didn't want to say goodbye. But I did, and the tears did eventually stop flowing. I will continue to be happy that there was someone like her in the world, and that I got to have her in my life.

16

TO BE CONTINUED

Although I was making positive moves in my own life and Bug was doing fabulous after her ordeal with the bullies, taking voice lessons, and singing her little heart out, I never stopped thinking that Savvi was still out there suffering. She had turned eighteen and as the law says she has a right to do, she refused help from any of us. She had been staying in the street and motels off and on and trying to find different places to stay. Although I had tried to bring her home, she could not stay clean, and therefore could not live at home. Bug was impressionable. The choices Savvi was making, and the people she brought around, were unsafe. I had to keep her away for our safety until she got clean, and it killed me.

I have had some moments of peace since Savvi's ordeal, but they always seem to get interrupted by her reality. She just keeps struggling no matter how many treatment centers, therapy sessions, or meetings with the team of people she has had in her life for years now. It has been an endless string of phone calls and e-mails week after week. Meeting her at random places to bring her clothes she left behind. I had just finished begging her to let her team help her, and get into treatment for her trauma and her addiction. I just had her skinny little hands in mine, holding them and not wanting to let go. She wouldn't stay, and I couldn't force her to. I had to watch her walk away back into the black hole she was living in. Helpless. That describes what I felt at that moment.

I had just received a call from someone who said Savvi sent them a picture of her face bruised with marks on her. They said it looked like she had been beaten. My heart sank. I thanked the person and texted Savvi asking her what happened and telling her I would come get her if she would just tell me where she was. My body went into ready mode as it had so many times in the past. But in her response to my texts she wouldn't tell me where she was. She said that it had just been a disagreement and that she was fine now. She told me to leave it alone, and she hung up on me. I was angry at her for saying that. How could I leave this alone? The same mother who fought for three years to save her could not be expected to do that. I remembered the times I have been beaten in the past and told people I was fine. I pictured her being hit and choked. I imagined, and even felt her pain. I felt the fear she must have been feeling. I also knew that she would numb those feelings with something and hoped she would survive the high. Knowing that she had been given heroin during her exploitation in order for them to keep her under control, the chances of her being safe during this time were very small.

As I thought about my child's pain, I began to cry. I cried for her, and for myself. I cried for all the girls and women who have felt and are still feeling that same pain. It isn't just a physical pain, it steals your soul and dignity. It crushes you and confuses the hell out of you. It brings question to your worth and that is usually the intent behind abuse. Regardless of the intent, the result is most assuredly the same. We become broken. It is excruciating to see my child live this.

I texted my friend, Kylie and told her what was happening. Kylie had become my friend when our paths had crossed because her daughter, Sahara, had also been bullied in the town we lived in. My Bug and her daughter had become the best of friends. They were inseparable, and the only time they left each other's side was when they went to school, as they attended different schools. I was so happy that Bug had finally found someone true to be her friend. I asked Kylie to ask around as she knew a lot of people. She and I had conversations all the time about Savvi. She knew that, even after all the things that had already happened, I was still living a nightmare with Savvi. She also saw how it affected Bug, and she was amazing to us. She loved Bug like her own child and recognized that she needed more than just me. She needed an extended family as well, to fill her life with as much love as possible. Kylie gave her that. She understood how difficult it was now that Savvi was eighteen, and I could no longer have the police search for her as I did when she was a minor. According to the law, she was an adult and, despite her history, they could not go and grab her like before.

I didn't even know where my baby girl was. I was basically on a need-to-know basis with Savvi. I would text or call her, and if she wanted to answer she would. If not, I wouldn't get to hear her voice. Even when she did answer, she never told me where she was, or who she was with. Even if I did find her, she wouldn't go with me; I know from experience that when in the throws of addiction, not even the most loving of parents can convince a person to come home or go to a program.

I called my daughter again, and she finally answered. I continued to beg her to tell me where she was, but she wasn't budging. I needed to get her to engage because I knew if she shut me out, she could go so deep underground that I wouldn't see or hear from her. Going underground means cutting off all their collaterals. The people who are their lifelines. When this happens, the chances of them coming back is not good. I changed my way of talking to her from mother to fellow abuse victim/survivor. I asked if she was in a safe place, and she said yes. My questions continued on as I requested information about what brought it on. She said she started it. (Of course she thought that.) I asked if he had any marks on him, and she said no. So I asked her, "You know that wasn't right, what he did to you, right?" She said it had never happened before, and I asked her if she wanted to go back, she said yes. That made me worry even more.

I asked her to send me the picture she had sent to the person who told me and she did. I was actually expecting much worse than what I saw, but it still took my breath away. She had a black eye, and scratches on her neck and a cut under her eye. I had never seen her this way, and I wanted to take action, but my hands were tied. With no location and no suspect, I couldn't do anything. She had also told me she didn't want any police involved. Even if I had I been able to get her location, she wouldn't have told the police anything. She wasn't in a place to want help. While the mother in me didn't understand why she wouldn't take the help, the history I had with that life forced me to realize why she was reluctant. I knew she was in the life for sure. Not that I hadn't known it before now, but this solidified it. You never call the cops when you are still living in that world and vulnerable to what can and will happen to you if you snitch. They could kill you. It happened all the time. The unidentified bodies that are found every day are not just overdoses, they are murders too. The freedom I experience from that life is only because I don't give those people an opportunity to have access to my life. I don't live that life anymore, so no one in it had any power over me. I won't allow it, but she, my baby, was still strongly involved in "the life," so she had to abide by the rules. My hands were tied, because unless she was willing to walk away from that world for good, any police involvement could put her life in danger. How would I feel if I caused her death?

Earlier that day I had been trying not to binge eat sweet things as was my habit every time I felt stressed out. Years before I had weighed over two hundred pounds, so it was very easy for me to gain weight. I had been through so much in my life that feeling stress didn't need to be triggered by anything in particular. All it took was a negative train of thought, and I was off and running so to speak. It was a lot like when I used drugs. All it took was one taste, one bite, and that was it. When I got the call from Savvi's friend, the thoughts began to creep in. I had started eating donuts and pecan shortbread from a café that Justice, who was still my boyfriend, and I spent a lot of time in. Those buttery pastries were going to make me need an entire wardrobe of new clothes, three sizes up from where I was now. I began binge eating them and filling my cheeks with their yumminess. Somehow it seemed they would take away my feelings and thoughts, but I didn't feel any better after inhaling two donuts, a pecan thing, and two cinnamon rolls that I had also baked. I just felt gross.

Sleepy from overeating, I got into bed. I needed to connect with her again somehow, so I texted her one last time. "Be safe tonight. I love you."

Lying in my bed, I began to breathe in slowly at a count of four, then out at the same count. I did this over and over slowly until I fell asleep. This was a technique I had learned in therapy. I used it at night and during the day just to ease the intense anxiety I had felt for so many years.

Before my eyes opened, I reached over to where my phone was plugged in, and I looked at it to see if there was any answer from my girl. There was. She said she loved me too, and had also sent another picture of her face. It broke my heart to see it. I messaged her back telling her that the picture made me sad and was she sure that she didn't want to go somewhere where she would be safe. She didn't answer. I tried to call her, but she didn't pick up.

I still don't know where she is, and I hope with all my heart that she can find her way out of this way of life. You see, it doesn't just end, the worrying, and the despair. I have somehow had to find a way of living and continuing to be OK all the while knowing that my child isn't safe. Once again, I was at the point where I was waiting for "The Call." I hope it never comes. I pray that she survives this.

My only recourse was to go in front of a judge and try to get what is called a guardianship. I had been discussing it with my attorney since her last treatment facility. She had always been willing to sign herself into treatment until now, and the law says she has to be willing to go. The only way without her consent was for a psychiatrist to commit her. During her most recent stay at the hospital, the psychiatrist said she was not committable despite the horrific things that happened to her when she was on the run, especially since her exploiter had left her with a heroin habit after forcing it on her in order to keep her under his control. This doctor said she had been doing just fine during her few weeks' stay at the facility. Of course she was doing fine, there were no drugs or predators in there! He was so clueless. All her issues began when she was left to her own decisions without any structure, and she needed to be in a locked facility so she couldn't leave whenever she wanted to. Without him committing her, she was free to leave as soon as she turned eighteen.

We had a meeting at the facility three weeks before her eighteenth birthday where I, her mentor, her therapist, and her mental health advocate begged her to agree to go into a locked facility to buy herself some time so she could get her head clear. While hope is great, we knew from her history of trauma that she was not ready to be on her own. It was my last chance before she became an adult for me to try to save my baby.

She listened quietly while we all talked and told her all the reasons we wanted her to sign herself into this long-term place. After everyone spoke, I spoke to her. I said, "Honey, please do this. You aren't ready to be out in the world. You need more treatment. You have been through so much, and you need help. You could die."

My voice shook, and I began to sob uncontrollably as I spoke. I wanted so badly for her to hear me. She said she was not going into another locked place, but would agree to go to a short-term program and by short term, I mean less than two weeks. It wasn't going to be enough. I was devastated, but powerless.

This is what sparked the talk of the guardianship, which basically gives me the right to say she cannot take care of herself or make decisions for herself, and force her into treatment. It would be a fight to get it, as they are usually given for parents of severely handicapped people, who physically or mentally cannot function. I am currently trying to get this in the hopes that if I find her, we can put her somewhere safe, like a detox, then a long-term program. For how long? I don't know. But it's my job to be there no matter what, and the concept of not being able to protect her doesn't make sense to me. I have to do everything I can to keep her alive. I can't give up on her.

17

MOTHER GRIZZLY

I have a strong maternal protective instinct. I feel an intense desire to seek out and destroy anyone who hurts my children. But...I have discovered that there are more powerful, effective ways to deal with abusers and bullies.

I have taken some shit for the way I choose to handle things when I go up against predators. I took a lot of criticism for my actions in connection with the bullying. I have been criticized *because* my girls had problems. One person made a disgusting comment to my friend Kara. She said, "What kind of mother has problems with both of her kids?" What a douche. I don't care what people like that think.

I fight for my kids. I do whatever has to be done to get them heard. When I learn that my children have been hurt, it feels as if my body has been struck by a bolt of lightning. At first I'm afraid that whatever is happening will be deadly. Then the adrenaline kicks in. I jump into action. I do whatever is necessary, moving on autopilot, not allowing myself to become frozen by fear or distracted by naysayers.

I pray, begging God to please let my kids be OK. This runs through my mind, over and over, until I am by their side. I hold and comfort them. I find out who has done what.

If I find out that their pain was inflicted by someone else, the anger starts to rise. I want to strike out, but I restrain myself. I channel the anger. I ask myself how to make this person, or people, accountable for what they've done. How can I expose them?

1) Was it a crime? Involve law enforcement.
2) Did anyone see it? Talk to witnesses.
3) How can I make them suffer in the most effective way possible?

These feelings do not go away for a very long time. I know that there are those who wish I would stifle such feelings. In fact, someone on a local website suggested that all the noise I was making online about Bug being bullied would not be helpful to her. “Good luck with using FB…I hope it helps your daughter; I bet it won’t.” This person knew that all the appropriate agencies were involved as well, but enjoyed criticizing a mother for her crying out anywhere and everywhere she could for help.

I have taught my girls to speak out, to point the finger directly at whoever is hurting them. To call out the evildoers. To shame them. Just as I *will* let the world know that wrong has been done.

Perhaps those people with the hush-hush attitudes have been threatened into silence at one time or another. Perhaps they are bullies or predators themselves.

I also hate people who are indifferent. F— you. Do something. Especially when it is a child who has been hurt. My God, I don’t get it. When I see a child hurt, something happens in me. I react. I call in the troops. Anyone who will listen. My heart goes out to the abused innocents. I wish I could be there to comfort every one of them.

How is it that parents can know that something has happened to their child and not act? F— that. That’s what the predators depend on. They need you to be afraid to talk.

Well, my way of dealing with abuse doesn’t have to be yours.

I have spent some time visiting my daughters in hospitals and group homes. I have seen too many young children and teenagers abandoned by their families. They are living in these treatment facilities, and no one comes to see them. Where are the loved ones? Is there no one to comfort them? I wish I had an army of moms to go to them. To hold them when they can't sleep at night. To tell them they love them. They need to know that someone cares about their existence. Trauma hurts. It's a lonely road to walk.

I remember when Savvi was in a group home. I went to visit her, and she told me she wanted to come home for a visit. The staff felt she was nowhere near ready. I cried and held her tight; she had no reaction. She didn't even hug me back even though I was sobbing. When I told her that she could not come home, she told me to get the f— out and not come back. This was painful, but I never stayed away. I kept chasing her every time she ran back to the life. Every time I got the call that she had run, I got on the phone with police, detectives, state police, The National Center for Missing and Exploited Children—any agency that I knew could get her picture and story out there. I spoke to a reporter and a private investigator. I fought for her life until she was ready to fight for it herself. Now she is living at home again after years of fighting for her life.

I will always fight for them, my babies. I cannot be any other kind of mother.

Doesn't everyone have this? The overwhelming need to protect all children. To let them speak out and to want to listen to them?

Sometimes I see children on the street or on the train, and I wonder if someone has been hurting them. Have they told someone? Or will they wait until they're thirty years old, as I did?

I know that people wonder, *Aren't you embarrassed?* Ahhh, the big question asked by those who do not understand my mind and all its workings. Yes, I am. I feel embarrassed, I feel shame, and I feel guilt. I have done things that I never wanted to do. I have had things forced on me that no one should experience. My actions have affected people that I did not want to hurt. I have those emotions, I am not those emotions. I have battled with all of these thoughts, and have chosen to move forward despite them. It has taken a lot out of me to think about these things, let alone write them down, reread them, type them out, then finally hand them over to someone else to read. Not only that, but I had no idea what people would say or think about my writing. Would they like it or hate it? Either way, it's all OK. It's my choice and that's what makes it special.

Knowing what I know about hearing someone tell their story and the power that has for someone else in the same situation, I would be even more ashamed had I not talked about these things. I do not, by any means, want to say that anyone who can't talk for themselves should feel badly. I mean that I know myself, and anyone who knows me will tell you that I have that drive in me, and the strength to help others. If I don't use that, then I have wasted my life. I was given a chance at a life I never thought I could have, but I want to share that with others. I can't keep it to myself. That wouldn't be right on my part. Besides, I would burst from having to keep quiet!

I almost feel angry when people tell me not to say anything, or not to discuss something. I have been reprimanded by some of my family for posting that Savvi was missing online. I don't care. It takes every eye and ear to find a child who is missing, and I always do what I believe will get results. I've also been told that I give too much information about my personal life, but guess what? It's my life, and I have to live in this body with all the things that have happened to it, so I think I'm going to continue doing what I need to do to get by. Love me or don't love me. This is who I am.

I have always asked my children how they felt about the routes I planned on taking to get them justice, and if they were comfortable with these measures. If they ever told me they were not happy with something, it didn't happen. It's easy to just go crazy and push forward without asking what a child feels in a sexual abuse or bullying situation, but it is crucial for them to keep some sort of control throughout the process of making things right. They have already been told they don't matter, or that they don't get a choice in what happens to them. It's up to us to treat them gently, and with understanding, not judgment.

I don't understand people who know something has happened to a child, but don't do anything. The child doesn't know how to fill out a police report or how to save evidence. They don't know how long DNA lasts in someone's body. Ugh! Wake up, people.

I also have a special hatred for mothers who allow their husbands or boyfriends to have sexual relationships with their children. Women who have been told by their children that something is happening, but not only do they do nothing, they allow it to continue. Because he is the only one paying the bills? You selfish bitches! You're disgusting, and I would love about ten minutes in a room with you. Not alone; I want people watching, so that you feel as humiliated as your child must feel. You'll get yours.

I was lucky. I didn't experience this myself, but I feel deeply for the children who do.

18

RESIDUALS

My God, the effect these things have had on me. How did I become this scattered, angry, suspicious person?

People, stop abusing one another! Your wives, your girlfriends, one another, other people's children. STOP IT NOW! I just want to be free of it all. To breathe, to sleep. To love freely. Without fear, without having to wear my armor.

I had developed a habit of living to please other people and making them happy so they didn't get mad and leave me. I've programmed myself to take from myself until there is nothing left because I gave it all away to another. I learned my very unhealthy way of survival street-side. I would starve my own soul to make someone else happy.

My mind is a circus. I clearly have abandonment issues. Sometimes I have hated my life. I hate the way my history has left me. I can't control myself. I have no control over the way my mind processes things. I can't stay asleep. Insecure, jealous, angry, afraid. Blocked from letting in any love at all. People who abuse have no idea what the aftermath of their actions is like.

Something else that angers me is the way some of the women who called me their friends behaved. Not in the beginning, because they were all there, but when it kept happening.

When Savvi's runs had started getting more frequent and longer, it was beyond devastating. The longest one was a month and three weeks. I felt my friends slipping away. My business was dying, and I was going broke. I owed so much money and couldn't pay the bills; I was canceling clients to deal with law enforcement or to spend nights at the hospital after Savvi had been found again. Despite the fact that certain people knew what was happening, I was being sued left and right.

I still remember a woman who had helped hang up posters the first time Savvi went missing. We became friends, but grew more distant when I didn't agree with some of her choices, and she didn't like my disapproval. Also, I had no time to hang out with her: one, because I was barely functioning and two, because I didn't want to be connected with what she was doing. She started asking me to pay some money that I owed her. I gave her what I could, but I didn't have much. It wasn't enough for her. She complained that I was spending money on getting my hair done and other things that helped soothe the pain I was feeling. Well, it was better than going back on the drink and drugs! The final straw was the puppy. My boyfriend had bought me a puppy to cheer me up. The woman started complaining about that. I finally told her to leave me alone, and she sued me. Unbelievable. How could she watch a mother in so much pain for so long and, out of anger and greed, take that woman into a court of law?

Someone else said that I was using my problems as an excuse and that I needed to learn a lesson. I think that was a disgusting thing to say. Especially since every person with children has to put his or her own life on hold. Any mother or father who was going through what I was would not be able to pay bills. She actually suggested I take out a loan to pay her! How does that make sense?

It was amazing how fast the bills began piling up, and the money stopped coming. I was drowning not only emotionally, but financially. What a nightmare. I didn't ask for this, but it happened, and I've dealt with it the best I can.

I feel that the women who abandoned and hurt me are traitors. They struck at me when I was at my weakest. Did they think I would stay silent about it? Wrong. They should be happy that I haven't revealed everything I could.

My war cry is always, "I have a right to..." because since childhood, I've kept quiet. So, I will no longer keep quiet about the things that hurt me. Not everyone has to agree with me and that's OK. After all, isn't that the way we create a happy life? We surround ourselves with those who are good for us and weed out the others. People change over time, and when it's time to go, it's time to go. Regardless of what that person thinks they have done for you or not.

Almost every unexpected noise startles me, especially at night. I wake up with my heart pounding, my breath ragged. I worry that someone has come to rape or kill me. Pain is imprinted on my brain, tattooed in my memory. The ink is my own blood.

For a long time, I could not trust anyone. Everyone's actions were suspicious. Even now, if I am going to interact with people, I need to plan carefully. I need to know exactly who is going to be there. If anything changes without warning, I can go completely over the edge. I have had happy moments, but these times were always shadowed by the fear that something foul was coming my way.

Is all this too strange? Who else feels this way? Are they alive, sober, are they clean? Are they aware that this is not a logical way of thinking?

I learned to think this way, to live this way, in order to protect myself. I needed protection from the outside world and anyone who wanted to come into my life for their own selfish reasons. This is a strong, strong pattern. It still kicks in every once in a while when I need it.

My view of the world has never been innocent. Well, maybe "never" is an exaggeration. There must have been a time after my first breath when everything was innocence. No intruders, just me in my mother's arms. Her looking at me, me looking at her. At this point, I don't know how long that lasted. I do know that I witnessed my mother being abused by my biological father before I was even two. Some of what has come up in my therapy sessions suggests that I might have been sexually abused even before the episode I remember, the molestation by the drunk. I have yet to remember anything. Maybe when I get a breather I will have the energy to look into it. But not yet. I'm tired.

19

WATCH ME FLY

I'm guessing that most people have not lived a life like mine. But I bet there are some who have suffered and survived, just as I did. I'd like to meet them.

I also know there are some still out there suffering and struggling to stay alive…or perhaps wishing that they were dead. I used to wish to just die, to end the misery, but despite all that I have endured; I am still standing. Standing strong in the face of whatever comes my way. Imagine me going from sleeping in basements and abandoned buildings to running my own business.

I had to struggle to stay sane. I'm not even sure that I did stay sane. Sometimes I think about having a drink. Not wanting it, really, but thinking about it, picturing myself ordering one…and then I remember what is on the other side of that drink. I know the night wouldn't end well.

I tell Justice, my boyfriend, that if I were to take a drink, he probably wouldn't see me for three days. I say it jokingly, but he knows and I know how much truth is behind those words. Am I immune from relapse? Absolutely not. But I pray that it never happens. I have fought my way through to this life and it would be devastating to my children and my loved ones if I gave up now. That would be the ultimate defeat.

Things have been so hard the last three years. Hard to sleep, hard to breathe. I don't know how I've been able to stand during all of it.

I had so much strength when I was standing up to all of the problems in my early life. But when my Savvi was hurt, it crushed me. When Bug was hurt, it almost killed me. At first I thought it was just because I was sober, clean, and wasn't self-medicating to deal with the pain. That is a part of it, but I think the feeling of a mother for her suffering child is more intense than any other. It is a feeling that crushes the soul. Rage comes from it. Tears come from it.

I held everything together for so long and once Savvi was safe, I was able to let it go, and I crumbled. I had said for so long, "I refuse to break." But I couldn't stop it this time. I had lost my spark. I was empty. It was a real fight to get myself back after everything that had taken place. I didn't drink or use, but my emotional state was bad.

I tried to claw my way out. I wanted to feel again. I wanted my personality and my fire for life back again. But at that time, I couldn't reach them. I was a mere shell of my former self.

There were so many reasons to give up, to shut down completely. I don't think people fully understand the aftermath of great suffering, the long-lasting scars that are easily irritated. I am devastated by an unwanted touch, a creepy look, by a guy making lewd comments about young girls.

I had been dating someone for five years when Savvi first went missing. He never once showed his face. When the police and detectives were coming in and out of my house, when we were rushing to the hospital when Savvi was found, everyone kept asking, "Where is ——?"

My guess is that he couldn't handle it—which meant he wasn't for me. I stand and I deal. The man in my life has to be able to do the same.

That said, there is someone who deserves to be mentioned. I call him Justice here, for his privacy's sake. He took the brunt of my anger when Savvi was missing, and I couldn't get my claws into the people I wanted to hurt. Despite my hurt and rejection, he waited. Waited for me to come around.

Bug likes to say we met because of her, which is partly true. Bug and I went to get ice cream at my friend's shop. When we went in, my friend was talking to Justice and one of his friends. She introduced us and the four of us all began talking. Laughing and being ridiculous. When we left, Bug said, "Mom, that military guy likes you." I was surprised that she noticed something like that and said, "Really?" Honestly, I had just been enjoying his company and didn't even notice his glances. Bug told me that "He kept coming over and wouldn't stop looking at you." That made me smile.

He contacted me a few days later; he got my number from my friend. Yes, ladies, he pursued me! Of course he didn't have to chase me for long because I quickly gave in to him, and we have pretty much been joined at the hip ever since.

For most of my life I have been unable to sleep soundly next to anyone. I would sleep on the edge of the bed, my leg almost hanging off the edge. I was hoping that my guy wouldn't try to cuddle me. I tried sleeping with a man in my first sober relationship, but it felt weird and unnatural.

The first night I slept with Justice was different. Savvi wasn't living at home yet, and Bug was with a sitter. I stayed at his house and when it was time to fall asleep (despite the fact that he practically suffocated me with his own body), I slept like a baby. It was amazing. I had a hard time staying asleep in my own bed and here I was, relaxed and feeling completely safe.

Justice put his hands on my shoulders and directed me through the storm. He stayed through all of it and never budged. No matter what I threw at him, he refused to leave. He has proven himself to me over and over again.

He has come to know me well. He knows that I am a wild one. Always have been, always will be. I will never be subservient, but I will always love deeply. I need to be who and what I am. I won't be anyone else. I tried doing that in relationships—in life in general—and I was miserable. The boyfriend I was seeing for the five years before Savvi ran away would say things like: Why are you wearing that? Don't lean on me. We're in a restaurant. We're in public—stop it.

I hated that. I felt so rejected because I had finally discovered that I loved touch and kisses and silliness.

Now I have discovered, after waiting for this my entire life, what it feels like when someone loves you. Period. Not wanting anything but love and respect in return.

It takes time for me to trust. Until now, I have never fully been able to do that. I was always with men who were hugging me and winking at the girl behind me. Or taking me to places where the girls they were sleeping with worked. So gross.

Back when I was living that twisted life, I was living with someone who claimed to be my boyfriend, but of course he was just another drug dealer who used me and lied to me. I was using at the time, so how could I have expected a healthy relationship? Anyway, I came home from God knows where, and went into the upstairs apartment. I could hear sex noises from the vent and knew it was him with someone. I went downstairs and banged on the door. He finally opened it and my best friend was sitting on the couch, fully dressed. But when she uncrossed her legs, I could see that the crotch of her pants was wet. The window was open and I peeked out there. Sure enough, there was a condom on the ground outside.

I went outside, picked up the condom, came in the house, walked up to him, and emptied the contents of the condom onto his face. Then I threw it at him. It hit him on his forehead and stuck there for a second before falling to the ground. I was avenged.

I never have to live that way again. What I have now is amazing. I haven't known this type of thing before. I've only recently known it, felt it returned, and known what it was for sure. Wow! It is so intense and I would say even intoxicating at times. Is he perfect? Nope. I know I'm not. But I'm hanging out with this feeling for a while. It feels so good. Will it last forever? I don't know. I guess we'll see.

There are times I wish that I could cut out those years in the life, but then I remember that I have lived through hell on Earth…get through that and you're golden, right? I also know that if one person with hungry ears hears my story and it helps them through it too, then it was all worth it.

I wish could go back to the time when I didn't constantly have a heavy feeling in my chest. The time when my mind was clear and I was still me, just me. The little girl who was molded into who I am today is still in there. Thanking me for fighting for her all this time.

I have had so many therapy sessions. I started going when Savvi's issues first began. I was being suffocated by the emotions that were emerging. They weren't just a mother's feelings of worry and fear for her child. They were years of pain and trauma that began pushing their way to the surface, mixing themselves with these new traumatic experiences. These feelings would not be denied. They haunted me even when I didn't want to feel them. I just wanted to be left alone, but I was being eaten alive from the inside out. I didn't want to go, but it was either that or allow myself to be destroyed. I couldn't function anymore.

My first visit was so difficult. Walking into that office was excruciating. Knowing that I would be baring my soul to someone that I didn't know felt unnatural. My habit was to feel pain and push it to the back of my mind, or so far down into my belly that I wouldn't think about it anymore. I sat in the chair across from a woman who would be listening to me for the next three years. Little bits and pieces would come out of my mouth. One at at a time, I released them from my body. I slowly became lighter, and over time I learned how to deal with the pain they caused when they showed themselves. What I learned during these sessions, was that all those years, I had been harming myself even further by not talking about the things that happened to me over the years. Acting like nothing was wrong with me, when in fact there was so much wrong with me that I was surprised I had survived it. Listening to myself saying some of these things out loud made me more aware of just how much I had been through. It made it real, and even shocked me. I was surprised I had survived it.

It took me an entire year of talking to her before I could cry in front of her. I believed that I had already cried every tear I had. I was also afraid that if I started crying, I would never stop. But that wasn't the case. The first time, my face crinkled up, and I thought I was going to pass out from the pressure in my head, but I was able to stop. I would cry for a few seconds at a time, and then it would go away. I discovered that it was possible for me to cry, recover, and move on with my day.

I fought my way back from these traumas with everything I had in me. I want to speak to anyone who thinks that this is the end for them. To anyone who feels that they can't go on another minute. You can, I'm telling you. You can. You take a breath, and you do it. Whatever it is. Leaving an abusive relationship, standing up for yourself, or (my personal favorite) standing up for your kids. It's about perseverance. You have it in you somewhere. You find it, you grab a hold of it with everything you have, and you make it happen. Overcoming fear is what I do, every day. I'm a fighter.

I want to see you survive. To know what it's like to live and not only get through it, but come out on the other side shining. You can. And you will.

16705815R00075

Made in the USA
Middletown, DE
20 December 2014